UP SHIT CREEK
IN A BARBED WIRE CANOE

[and how to cope with it]

Your book Shit Creek is an extremely serious book masquerading as a funny one. It is like Leunig's work, a textbook for life. I wish I had owned a copy 30 years ago.

— Liz Hicklin, author of *Kiss and Cry*
and *Limerence*

It's been a ripper of a read! I really liked it. It seems ambitious to canvass most of life in around 100 pages, but it reads like a distillation of truths from your professional and personal experience. Wise and practical. And because it is chatty and funny, it is easy to read. To cover all relationships, work, children, teenagers, depression, self-esteem and the entire parasympathetic nervous system in a short book is quite an achievement!

— Jeanette Woods, author of *A Voice For Veronica*
and *Living for Shalom*.

Witty and wise and practical. It reminds me, in a good way, of 'You're terrible, Muriel!'

— Rob Gerrand, co-author of *Rewrite Your Life!*
and *Rewrite Your Relationships!*

You explain so much in a clear, concise manner, making it easy to understand. The breathing techniques, BOB, FOB, I have never had them explained to me like that in the past. You have helped me way more than you will know, and I thank you.

— Ally Jaks

Also by Muriel Cooper

Lucid

The Tiger and the Bridge

UP SHIT CREEK
IN A BARBED WIRE CANOE

[and how to cope with it]

Muriel Cooper

NORSTRILIA PRESS

NORSTRILIA PRESS
11 Robe Street, St Kilda 3182 Australia
norstriliapress.com

Cover image used with the permission of the late Michael Leunig.

Cover design by David Grigg
Book design by David Grigg
Typeset in Gill Sans and Adobe Garamond Pro.

ISBN 978-1-7638516-0-3 (paperback)
ISBN 978-1-7638516-1-0 (eBook)

Introduction

A barbed wire canoe (AI generated)

If you've ever been up shit creek in a barbed wire canoe, you'll know that you long for a way out. You're depressed, your bum hurts, and you feel like a fool. A paddle would do you no good at all. Sometimes, you feel you can't talk to anyone about it. What you need are strategies, which is what this book gives you. You probably don't need a long, thick, complicated book (this one is not – I aimed to do it in around a hundred pages), and you could probably do with a laugh or at least a smile (I hope you get one here).

Shit has become an everyday word. Like the 'F' word, it is now in the common vernacular as a way to express ourselves. Usually, nobody is offended (well, not much anyway, and if they're too 'poopy' about it, they're a shit). If things do give you the shits, this little book can be beneficial to help you cope with shit, whether it's an accident, stress, anxiety, depression, a shitty relationship, irritating relatives, shit at work, or shit in the world at large. This is only an introduction to coping with shit. If it doesn't help and you're not dealing with it, get help.

I hope this helps you to have a relatively shit-free life. Thanks to all my friends, family, and clients who gave enthusiastic help and advice.

Another barbed wire canoe (AI generated)

I made this around 100 pages because when you're going through shit, you might not want to wade through too much description. You'll find heaps of supplementary stuff in the appendices and on my website, The Talking Room.

Warning: By now, you should know that this book uses the word shit many times, as well as other curse words. If that makes you uncomfortable, then this book might not be for you (or look up some of my very serious web articles on www.talkingroom. com.au)

Every effort has been made to attribute images and material in this book.

The book's complete table of contents is coming up if you wish to look up a specific topic.

Contents

Why swearing can be good for you   1

The new meaning of shit   2

When you are up shit creek in a barbed wire canoe   3

How to get your shit together   4

    Here is a simple method for assembling your shit   4

    Categorise your shit   5

    When should I give a shit?   5

    How to know when and when not to give a shit. Summary.   8

Shit happens   10

    Can I stop shit from happening?   10

    The shit has hit the fan – shit is happening now   11

    Here's what to do when the shit hits the fan   12

    'I'm a shit magnet'   14

    When you feel like shit/feel shithouse   14

    How to feel better when you feel like shit and why it works   15

    'This gives me the shits' – 'I'm over this shit' – 'I don't need this shit' – 'I'm sick of this shit!'   18

    What to do when you're sick of that shit   18

    When you're on the shit list - treated like shit / not approved of / not belonging   19

    What is a shit/shithead?   21

    How not to be a shit/shithead   21

    How to deal with a shit/shithead   22

    It's a shit fight (how to deal)   23

    Shit fights happen. Here's how to cope.   23

    Muriel's 5 P's   23

    Know your shit   24

    Being full of shit   25

    Bullshit (also known as horseshit) or bull for short   26

    Bullshit meter   27

    Being scared shitless (or shit scared)   27

    Losing your shit/going 'ape shit.'   29

    How to cope with losing your shit   30

    Accept that shit (not reacting)   31

    Let go of that shit   31

    How to let go of old shit   32

How to let go of new shit (that just happened) 33
You feel like a piece of shit – (not worthwhile) 33
How to cope with feeling like you are not worth jack shit 34
When you look like shit 34
What to do when you look like shit 35
When you talk shit (Can't communicate) 36
How to communicate better 36
The assertiveness formula 37
You can do that shit – self-confidence. 38
Don't put shit off (procrastinate) 39
What to do about procrastinating 40
Get rid of that shit! (De-cluttering) 40
A piece of shit/a heap of shit and what to do when it is 42
Your work is a piece of shit 42
You're a piece of shit! 42
How to know when someone is shitting you 43
'You're shitting me.' 44
When you're dropped in the shit/been shat on from a great height 44
How to recover (from being dropped in the shit) 45
People treat me like shit 46

Miscellaneous shit 47

How to cope with major shit 56
Stress 56
Knowing about stress 57
What to do about stress 58
The importance of diet in stress management 59
Shower Visualisation for stress (and other shit) 60

Anxiety/panic and what to do about it 61
Social anxiety 62

Depression 64
Some strategies to deal with depression 65

Shit at work 67
Watch out for these four major workplace stressors: 67
What to do 68

Shit in relationships 71
How to head off a shitty breakup 72
What to do when suddenly, everything about them shits you 72
You haven't learned how to fight 73
Not thinking as a couple 73
Neglecting your friendship relationship 74
Trust and intimacy are low 75
R.E.S.P.E.C.T. 75
Stay attracted to each other 76
Muriel's 3 Cs of relationships 77
How to rescue a deadshit relationship 77

Parenting shit 78
    Parenting young children 79
    Parenting teenagers 81
Appendices 87
Desiderata 87
Rules for good communication with yourself (and others) 89
How To Say No (to unfair requests and demands) 92
Muriel's Simple Brain Training Rules 94
Relaxing Exercises 96
    Meditations 96
    Muriel's 'Looking, breathing and letting go' meditation. 97
    Progressive Muscle Relaxation 98
Breathing exercises for S.A.D. (Stress, Anxiety, and Depression) 100
    The Vagal breath 100
    Abdominal breathing 100
    Breath, step back and let go (for reactivity) 101
How to Get a Better Night's Sleep 102
Visualisation Exercises for Stress, Anxiety Depression 105
    Emotional memory exercise 105
    Favourite/safe place visualisation 105
    Come out of the cave exercise 106
Physical exercise 107
Acknowledgements 108
Bibliography, References and Further Reading 109

Why swearing can be good for you

'That can't be true,' I hear you say. 'Only vulgar people who can't put two words together swear.' Honestly, the positive and therapeutic effects of swearing have been studied. Swearing can not only relieve stress and pain; it can make you stronger. It deactivates the emotional centres in the brain, so it's distracting. Laughing is great for this, too; it encourages endorphins, so swearing and laughing at the same time while having a tooth pulled could be the bomb. It won't be the first time the dentist's heard it.

Look – when you bash your thumb with a hammer, do you say, 'Oh, golly gosh'? No, you swear. It's cathartic. You can yell it out, you can whisper it under your breath, but when you're up shit creek, give in to your inner curser. It can get you through a lot of shit. Like Colin Firth, who plays future King George VI in the movie *The King's Speech*, who didn't stutter when he swore. As speech therapist Lionel Logue (played by Geoffrey Rush) says,

'Defecation flows trippingly from the tongue.'

You don't want to overuse it; otherwise, it loses its power and impact. Save it for when you genuinely need it, then let it rip. It can do you a power of good.

The new meaning of shit

Shit is not just plain old shit anymore – it has infinite variety and has become a way to express how we feel about:

- People   (He/she/they is/are a shit).
- Things   (It's a heap/piece of shit)
- Issues   (It's a shitty situation/it's all gone to shit)
- Us   (I feel like shit)

It can be a convenient word when you want to vent your feelings, and it's generally less offensive than the 'F' word and, certainly, the 'C' word, which is right up there on the offensiveness scale.

> *'Shit is the tofu of cursing and can be moulded to whichever condition the speaker desires. Hot as shit. Windy as shit. I myself was confounded as shit...'*

> — David Sedaris

When you *are* up shit creek in a barbed wire canoe

With or without a paddle, you're in trouble. You're not coping, stressed, anxious, depressed, or being bullied; there's shit in your relationship; you are in the shit. For whatever reason you are in this situation or feel this way, you need to take action. It doesn't have to be huge – small steps are fine. If you do nothing, make it a *decision* to do nothing; don't sit there because you feel overwhelmed or paralysed by the situation or feelings. Don't just sit there wallowing in shit. What you need is a strategy, and there are many in this book. You could also consult:

A business adviser/accountant/lawyer

A psychologist

A medical practitioner

A coach

A teacher/trainer

Whatever you do, do *something*. Stress can make you vulnerable to poor decisions (see the section on stress), so don't make major, life-changing decisions. Just decide what you're going to do next, big or small.

How to get your shit together

It is one of the mysteries of the universe that one's shit often ends up spread all over the place (metaphorically speaking). I am forever gathering up my shit and working on it.

Here is a simple method for assembling your shit

- Make a list of your shit
- Plan how to deal with your shit. Remember, the brain loves a plan, especially Stressed, Anxious and Depressed people (please note this will now be referred to as S.A.D)
- Prioritise your shit
- Try to clean up a little bit of your shit every day

Here's an example of my own shit list:

This is giving me the shits	What I'm going to do about it
This is the third day I've put off that project.	Think of a way to reward myself for starting the project and do ten minutes of it. Procrastinating makes you feel like shit.
My husband, H.B. hangs the ironing up on the frame of the laundry door where the spare toilet is and I keep knocking my head on it when I go to said toilet	Instead of yelling, 'This gives me the shits!' when it happens *I will take a deep breath*, also I will *assertively* ask H.B. to hang his ironing somewhere else – hence avoiding the possibility of my losing my shit.

If you keep an eye on your shit, you have a better chance of dealing with it, so don't let your shit get out of hand.

Categorise your shit

There are two categories of shit.

1. I give a shit

2. I don't give a shit

Life will be less shitty if you know when and when not to give a shit.

When should I give a shit?

- When you genuinely care about a *person/s*, and they are in the shit
- When you genuinely care about an *issue* that is giving you the shits (e.g., who is in government/corruption/dogs in hot cars/global warming.)
- When you genuinely care about a *thing* that is giving you the shits (e.g., a sick plant/your car has broken down/your yacht has run aground)

If you give a shit about any of these – then do something about it – take action.

If you genuinely *don't* care, but you pretend to give a shit just because you think you *should*, because: 'What will people think?' Then beware of 'I:

Should

Must

Have to

Ought to.'

These can be crippling and give you the shits big time. You might think you're going to give someone the shits if you say *no* when you think they want you to say yes, so you say yes, even though it gives you the shits, and you know you're going to regret it. Or you agree with someone because you think you *should*.

For example, a friend says:

'Don't you think it's awful what Brad did to Angel?'

You – thinking to yourself – *'I don't give a shit about Angel; she was mean to Brad, and I think it's great that he cracked the shits with her.'*

Instead, because you want to look like you agree with your friend so she won't be put out, you say:

'Oh yes, Brad's a real shit for doing that to her.'

Trust me, this is a time when to *not* give a shit about what your friend thinks. Be true to yourself, stand up and say what you *really* think and not what your friend wants you to. Who cares if they crack the shits? They'll let you have your own opinion if they're truly your friend.

Also, give people the benefit of the doubt; your friend might not know Angel was mean to Brad. Risk it and tell them.

But isn't that gossip? Of course, it is, but gossip is the social glue that keeps us together.

Also, it's all in the telling. Here's how to tell it:

'I don't agree because I know for a fact that Angel was mean to Brad, so in this case, I'm supporting him for not putting up with it.'

Notice that you're using 'I' language, focusing on Angel's *behaviour* rather than on her, and sticking to what you know are the facts. You're assertive in stating our point of view, which makes it information rather than gossip, which is often unfounded rumour and malicious.

Is it ever okay to pretend to give a shit?

Take employment, for instance. If you're offered a job that you don't honestly want, *appearing* to give a shit about the job when you don't might be diplomatic and get you the job. But think again. If you end up in a job you don't want just to please someone, it might not be worth it, and the job mightn't last. Of course, if you're desperate and need the money to survive, you might accept that it's a shitty job, and you'll hang in there until you can get something better.

Doing it because your friends are. You might think: '*All my friends are giving money to this charity, but I don't actually give a shit about this issue.*' You could pretend to give a shit and give them time and/or money just because you think you *should* and not because you want to, and then feel resentful. Instead, find a charity you *do* give a shit about and give money to them.

If you genuinely do give a shit about a person, issue, or thing, and you *don't* take action to help, this can give rise to guilt and remorse. These are often unnecessary emotions that are stressful. So, give a shit and do the right thing, but do it on your terms and be assertive bout the people-pleasing.

Guilt can be a useful emotion because it stops us from doing things that are illegal or give people the shits. It makes us feel so bad at the thought of doing it that we don't, and we won't do it again in the *future*. That's what guilt is for. Not for ruminating and stressing over things in the past you have no control over and can't do anything about.

'Just keep moving forward and don't give a shit about what anybody thinks. Do what you have to do for you.'

— Johnny Depp – probably before he got into trouble for bringing his dogs Pistol and Boo into Australia.

How to know when and when not to give a shit. Summary.

When you *genuinely* don't give a shit about that

- Person

- Issue, or

- Thing

then don't be guilted into giving a shit just because you're afraid of being disapproved of (remember, no should).

Learn to say no. Learn to be assertive (see How To Say No in the appendices).

Learn how to not give a shit in an assertive, pleasant, guilt-free way.

If you don't give a shit but *pretend* you do to avoid guilt or to make someone like or approve of you? Revelation! They're probably completely unaware of your deceit; you've guilted yourself for nothing! More fool you. That shit you gave was a waste of time, emotion, and money. You should not have given one.

Do be true to yourself. But – if you don't give a shit, but it would be hurtful to say so, then don't say it. For example, if you don't give a shit about your grandma, but it would be cruel to tell her so, be kind and pretend.

Exercise for knowing when to give and when not to give a shit

Don't think it! Ink it! Writing things down gets them out of your head.

Things I don't give a shit about	Things I do give a shit about

'I just stepped in shit, and now I've got political rhetoric all over my shoes.'
— Jarod Kintz, *This Book Has No Title*

Shit happens

In a review of Fred Shapiro's work The Yale Book of Quotations *in 2006,* The New Yorker *critic Louis Menand stated that it is 'extremely interesting' that the phrase 'Shit happens' was introduced to print by Connie Eble, in 1983, in a publication identified as 'UNC-CH Slang'. So 'shit happens' has been around for around thirty-odd years.*

It can be infuriating when someone trivialises the shit you're in by nonchalantly saying, 'Oh well, shit happens.'

'Excuse me, but this shit is happening to *me*,' you grumpily say to yourself. 'What a shit!'

If you deliver this platitude to someone when they've been hurt or received bad news – then you're a shit. Any way you look at it, 'Oh well, shit happens' is a brush-off phrase best reserved for people you don't know very well or politicians. Otherwise, it could get taken personally. Of course, if you're saying it to *yourself*, then that's fine.

> *Shit happens*
> *You can learn how to cope with it*
> *It passes*
> *Life is not all shit*

— Muriel

Can I stop shit from happening?

No, you cannot. Shit happens, and we build resilience because we have to work our way through and get over shit. If shit never happens to us, if and when it does, we are often in trouble because we don't know how to deal. We haven't built resilience. If you haven't had the opportunity to build resilience because you've had a charmed life (lucky you), you can cope much better when shit finally happens to you by learning how to deal with it in advance. Like the good Boy or Girl Scout, be prepared.

Even if you've had shit happen and survived, having a plan to deal with further shit when and if it happens is an excellent idea (remember, the brain loves a plan). Despite all your precautions and experience, shit can still happen and probably will.

'The best-laid schemes of mice and men gang aft agley.'
—Robert Burns

The shit has hit the fan – shit is happening *now*

Your car has broken down in the middle of nowhere in the middle of the night.

There actually is a tiger about to jump on you.

You have made a terminal error at work or in your essay/thesis/exam.

There's nothing left in your bank account

You've been found out/sprung.

The shit has hit the fan. It's acute stress time – fight or flight.

Here's what to do:

'Don't panic.'
(On the cover of 'The Hitchhikers Guide to the Galaxy)

I know it's easy for me to say. Your survival brain (roughly at the back, so for convenience, I call it Back of Brain, or BOB) will want you to panic. That usually involves cutting off anything to do with your rational brain (in the front) and making you run around like Chicken Little.

11

BOB does not want you to think, 'Ooh, what a nice tiger' – it wants you to *react*. In this case, 'Run away, run away!' (Monty Python), or fight like hell. In the case of the tiger, this is not recommended unless you're participating in an initiatory ritual that involves vanquishing a tiger. Good luck with that one.

Here's what to do when the shit hits the fan

Take a Vagal breath (ideal for panic – the Vagus nerve, the biggest nerve in the body, regulates the fight/flight response)

- *The Vagal breath*: take a *deep* breath, slowly counting to three… hold it for three seconds, counting to three…, and let it out *very* slowly. It needs to last at least six to eight seconds. This balances the autonomic nervous system and can help reconnect the Back of the Brain/survival brain (BOB) with the Front of Brain/rational brain (FOB) and help you regain some control and perspective. Now, take a mental step back and take another breath. Do as many of these as you need to calm down.

Recent research indicates that when you have panicky anxiety, nine breaths is optimal—otherwise, as many as you need to calm down.

Reassess the situation and get perspective

Assess the situation from every angle before you take action (unless it *is* a tiger. In which case, fight or run like hell). Take your time. Stress fools with your ability to think and make decisions, so you don't want to do anything rash. Take. Your. Time, and don't let other people pressure you. Do not make any hasty decisions. You might come to regret a decision made under acute stress. Wait until you calm down and can get perspective on the shit you're in.

Make a plan

The brain loves a plan. Without one, you will continue to run around like Chicken Little as the brain catastrophises and flip-flops all over the place, going over a hundred different scenarios. The brain spends about 80% of its time assessing threats. Most of these are lightning-fast calculations of which you are entirely unaware. It's what the brain does best: make up your mind for you in a hundred ways all at once. Usually, this is a good thing; for example, you don't want to have to think about everything you do. The brain functions seamlessly to make all those little decisions for you. But in a crisis, this remarkable ability of the brain can be confusing and paralysing. Its instructions are (in one millisecond):

Fight – argue, shirtfront, punch in the nose. Not recommended.

Flight – run, avoid, be passive-aggressive.

Freeze – (let's not move. Maybe it won't see us).

Fawn (Shrink ourselves physically and become submissive).

None of these is a plan. It's a *reaction*.

Decide to do at least one thing, even if it's to take a Vagal breath (or two or nine) and do nothing at all right now. Then, make a more detailed plan.

Follow the plan

Write it down. Stick to it. Plans can be flexible.

As I was thinking about writing this little book, there was a story in the news about a woman at the Toronto Zoo who jumped a fence in the tiger enclosure to get her hat. Admittedly, there was a fence between her and the furious tiger, but it goes to show how BOB, the survival brain, can be overcome by rash actions, extreme foolishness, impulsiveness, and

irrational thinking. Before you follow her example, I
suggest a few Vagal breaths.

'I'm a shit magnet'

Sometimes you feel like you've got a big sign on your
forehead that says 'Shit on me' because shit keeps
happening one lousy way after another. It's that 'run of
bad luck' no one ever wants to have (unless you're a
masochist).

Don't perpetuate that shit with a negative,
pessimistic, shitty attitude. Sometimes shit happens
because we make it a self-fulfilling prophecy. 'Nothing
good ever happens to me; my life is shit and will always
be shit.' This will not attract the opposite. If you want
roses, then think about roses, not shit.

Remember, sooner or later, that shit will pass.
The sign will come off your forehead.
Persist – keep going.

— Muriel

Never give up, never give up – never give up
— The Dalai Lama

Never, never, never give up
— Winston Churchill

Never give up, for that is just the place that the tide
will turn.

— Harriet Beecher Stowe

Hang in there

— (me again)

When you feel like shit/feel shithouse

Sometimes there's a reason. Sometimes there's no
reason. You can't pinpoint any specific cause. You
simply feel like shit. You didn't do anything; it isn't fair,
but there it is:

'It wasn't fair, but what is? Life is a crap carnival with shit prizes.'

— Stephen King, *Mr Mercedes*

Always remember that reason or no reason, it rarely lasts; it passes; *it's temporary!* Accept it and wait to feel better. It's OK to feel like shit sometimes (see, accept that shit – not reacting). You accept having the flu, don't you? You know you're going to feel like shit for a couple of weeks at least, and you do whatever you can to feel better and wait for it to go away. Emotional shit is no different.

Remember, you have the right to *do whatever it takes to feel better* (as long as you don't hurt anybody).

Imagine how you're going to feel when all this shit stops – how good it's going to feel – what you're going to be doing – who you're going to be with – where you're going to be. Then *positively* ruminate, visualise and look forward to the shiny future to come when all this shit has passed and go over and over it in the same way you do when you negatively ruminate – like a mantra. *

Negatively ruminating only makes you feel like shit.

'Every day, in every way, I'm getting better and better.'

— Believed to be the first affirmation by Émile Coué

Coué was a French psychologist and pharmacist who invented affirmations in the early 1900s. They became a craze because they work—ask Louise Hay.

How to feel better when you feel like shit and why it works

It's good to find out what works specifically for you, but generally, these things can make you feel better.

• A good night's sleep

> One hundred percent the most important thing you can do. The basic rules are to have a

15

routine, keep your room cool, quiet and dark, and breathe in for three and out for three, saying 'one' on the outbreath. See appendix 'How to get a better night's sleep.'

- Being near water or having a bath or shower

- Going for a walk or exercise

    Exposure to nature can decrease your stress by up to 25%, and a brisk walk can give you endorphins and dopamine (feel-good brain chemicals). Exposure to the sun can also give you a good daily dose of Vitamin D, which is very important for mood.

- Meditating and mindfulness

    See appendix 'Muriel's looking and breathing exercise.'

- Talking to a friend (or a helpline)

    Human contact is crucial for most people. We have language to replace physical grooming. It's soothing and reassuring.

- Watching a movie

    Action and distraction take your mind and brain off things.

- Listen to your happy music mix

    Music is so good; it's a form of therapy all on its own.

- Hug something (a pet, a person, yourself)

    Touch is hugely important. It's tantamount to physical grooming. You will get a nice burst of endorphins even if you hug *yourself*.

- Write down how you feel

    It's a well-known fact that writing things down and getting them out of your head helps stop worry and rumination.

- Find something funny

Laughter is the best medicine because it gives you those endorphins.

- Look at happy pictures
- Make a cup of tea (tea contains Theanine – a feel-good substance)
- Be grateful (remember it could be worse)

Writing three things you're grateful for before bed is proven to reduce S.A.D (Stress, Anxiety, Depression)

- Look up into the sky

Blue light switches off melatonin and perks you up, especially first thing in the morning.

- Vitamins and minerals, especially vitamins B, C, D and Magnesium
- Give yourself a motivational talk

What you say to yourself is more important than what you say to others. Be self-reassuring, self-encouraging, self-compassionate and self-empathetic.

- Lift your posture – lift your head up, open out your chest and look the world in the eye

Your body language, like self-talk, can send reassuring messages to your brain. A simple thing to do is lift your collarbones towards the ceiling.

- Smile for no reason

Make sure you do the crinkly eyes thing. Moving all the muscles of your face with a smile gives you endorphins.

- Generate compassion/love.

This is something you know makes you feel love or happiness. Feel compassion for people and all living things. Send it out there. Also, feel compassion for yourself.

17

There are scientific reasons why these things work, and I've given you some of them (you can look them up, or you'll find books about them in the bibliography at the end), but just do them. When you do, you feel better and look more confident.

As Tyler Durden says in the movie 'Fight Club,'
'If you feel like shit, everyone you hate wins.'

'This gives me the shits' – 'I'm over this shit' – 'I don't need this shit' – 'I'm sick of this shit!'

Sometimes we put up with shit for far too long. Shitty relationships, a shitty job, a shitty relative, even a shitty friend.

Why do we put up with shit? Because we think we *should* (there are those shoulds again), otherwise, we'll be a bad person/partner/friend. Or we don't want to lose them/it, even if they are shitty. We hang in there, hoping that shit will change. Hey, persistence is one of my top five qualities (the other three P's out of my four P's being patience, positivity, perspective and being present), but when you've been worn down by a shitty person/situation or thing that is obviously *not* going to change, it's time to bite the bullet and either change things or get rid of that shit.

What to do when you're sick of that shit

- Accept that it won't change unless you take action. You might need to move on
- Be brave. Working on or getting out of a shitty relationship or job takes courage
- It *will* be stressful. Look after yourself (see Stress and When you feel like shit)
- Accept the bad feelings. You probably *will* feel shitty (see Accept that shit)
- Plan, Plan, Plan! You need a firm plan, even if it's

just how you're going to deal with your emotions, thoughts and behaviours; otherwise, BOB (back of brain) will panic

- Set goals for what you want to move towards
- Be assertive (see When you talk shit/can't communicate)
- Get help and support from family and friends
- Remind yourself frequently that you are doing the right thing (we don't like change, and your brain will want to pull you back into what it thinks is the comfort zone even though it's uncomfortable there. Resist backsliding!)

'Life is 10 percent what happens to you and 90 percent how you respond to it.'

— Charles Swindoll

When you're on the shit list - treated like shit / not approved of / not belonging

Being on a person or an organisation's shit list not only feels shitty, but it is also very threatening to our survival brain (BOB). It means (in a tribal sense) that we get less food, less water, less protection, and we get shoved to the edge of the group and get picked off by the tiger.

It's life and death stuff to BOB. Being on a list of anything that isn't good is threatening.

Like:

- Not being in the cool group.
- Your boss has you in their sights.
- You feel like your partner has it in for you.
- Not being included in the lunch crowd. Teenagers, particularly, feel terrible angst when

they're on the shit list since belonging to a peer group is crucial at this age.

Being on the shit list might mean you're being discriminated against, and that's illegal. If the boss doesn't like you, and they want to find a way to get rid of you – which they might do, it must be legal. You have rights. If you're not being included because you're 'different,' there are laws about that. We have anti-discrimination laws. Tell someone – report it to your boss, the head teacher or the police.

If a group is not including you because they're just being shits, well, there's no law against being a shit. Perhaps you need to improve the quality of your friends and relationships. To humans, there are few things scarier than being on the shit list.

> *'Whoever said, "When life gives you lemons, make lemonade" is on my shit list. What if you don't have the recipe?'*
>
> — (Muriel, and yes, you can quote me on this).

P.S. An Australian Prime Minister found himself in the shit during the horrendous bushfires of 2019/20 when, during the crisis, he took a holiday to Hawaii. He was in the shit when he turned up at a fire-affected town only to be told by locals to 'fuck off'.

He was in the shit once again when women protested about how they were treated in the Canberra bubble and again when the rollout of the vaccine for Covid-19 went terribly wrong. If you don't want to end up in the shit, it might be wise to do the right thing or don't make any promises you can't keep, even if you're a politician.

What is a shit/shithead?

Being a shit is being:

    Rude

    Thoughtless

    Hurtful

    Aggressive

    Abusive

    Manipulative

    Deceitful

    Despicable

    Criminal

    Behaving stupidly

Nobody likes a shit.

How not to be a shit/shithead

Be:

    Polite

    Thoughtful

    Try not to hurt people

    Be assertive, not aggressive (Being assertive is being firm, standing up for yourself, but not hurting people (or yourself).

    Don't be abusive or manipulative

    Be honest, tolerant and truthful

    Don't break the law

    Don't do stupid things (even when you're drunk – it's no excuse for being a shit).

How to deal with a shit/shithead

Having outlined the characteristics of a shit, it is useful to know how to deal with one.

Dealing with a shit by being a shit back is grounds for conflict, arguments, and bad relations. This achieves nothing.

- First, analyse the shit/shithead – decide what tactics they are employing – then formulate a plan for dealing with them. Write it all down. Remember — the brain loves a plan.

- Second, know how to be assertive. This is a (usually) fail-safe way to deal with a shit. It might take practice, but it builds your self-confidence. Learn assertiveness; read a book; take a class. See the appendix 'Assertive communication.'

- Third, know your rights and get help (if the shit is being abusive, for example). If your shit is at work, call your union or government fair work body, or take it up with the HR department

- Fourth, ridiculise that shit/shithead by imagining them dressed up as a cartoon character, Wylie Coyote, or Miss Piggy. Every time you see them or think of them this way, you ridiculise them. This makes BOB/survival/stress brain laugh at them instead of fearing them. It's well worth a try. Wave your imaginary Harry Potter wand and shout, 'Ridiculise!' (Maybe not out loud)

- If the shit is merely being an idiot, do not react. Walk away from the shit.

Putting up with a shit indefinitely is hugely stressful, anxiety-provoking, and depressing. Take action.

It's a shit fight (how to deal)

Definition of shit fight:

'A great, messy struggle, such as a freeway at rush hour or registration at a large university."

— (Urban Dictionary)

Boy, did the university registration example strike a chord with me? It's a massive shit fight involving long queues for every subject. You get to the table, and you haven't got the correct paperwork. Grrr!

Shit fights happen. Here's how to cope.

If you know it's going to be a bit of a shit fight, plan ahead.

- Use Muriel's 5 P's (coming up next)
- See 'Losing your shit/going 'ape shit"; 'Accept that shit' (don't react), and 'Miscellaneous shit' in this book
- Remember, 'It passes.' Everything is temporary
- How can I pass the time until the shit fight's over (listen to the radio, chat to someone in the queue, call a friend.)
- Breathe and try to relax
- If it's dangerous or illegal, call the police

Muriel's 5 P's

I formulated these years ago, and they have been a tried and true method for dealing with shit in my life and the lives of my clients.

1. Patience

    Have patience with yourself and with the process. Don't over-pressure yourself or put shit on yourself.

2. Persistence

   Keep going; keep going, keep going. Do not give up. You will get there.

3. Positivity

   Be as positive as possible – remember, the brain is not wired to be positive; it's wired to see threats. Take time to build up positive trains of thought. That doesn't mean you have to be 'happy, happy' all the time. You're allowed to feel sad and bad. Feel the feeling, name it (this joins the front and back brains), and let it go. Do the best you can.

4. Perspective

   Get your perspective right. Come from the 'Me' perspective (Mindful Awareness – keep an eye on yourself). Remember, you are not your brain; you are what is noticing what your brain is doing. Also, do not Catastrophise, alwaysise, historicalise, futurise, mind read. (See appendix 'How to communicate with yourself and others'). Getting things in perspective helps BOB (survival brain) to relax.

5. Presence

   Be in the moment of now – be present – right in this moment when, usually, nothing catastrophic is happening. Don't historicalise and don't futurise.

Know your shit

'He (or she) knows their shit' is one of the highest compliments we can hear when it's said about *us*. We spend a lot of time learning shit at school, TAFE (Technical and Further Education), University, and work.

One thing I have learned is that not knowing your

shit can be ultra-stressful. Here are two examples from my own experience. I started a new talk radio current affairs program and suddenly realised I knew jack shit about politics. It was a horrifying moment. Luckily, I had a generous work colleague who was willing to mentor me until I learned my political shit.

Another occasion where I lost my shit about not knowing my shit was when I was asked to conduct a class on Media and Public Relations at a major technical college because the lecturer had fallen ill. I arrived to find there were no lesson plans and no course materials, and the classes started in a few days. I ran around like Chicken Little, trying to scrape together something that looked like I knew my shit. I made it by the skin of my teeth, but it took a few years off my life.

So not knowing your shit can be incredibly stressful and embarrassing.

It is worth taking time and effort to know your shit. Trying to bullshit your way through can be extremely stressful. If you're misled about what shit you need to know, ask for time to get your shit together. Then, work through it systematically until you are reasonably confident.

If you want to be taken seriously, know your shit. Nobody wants to be called 'shit for brains.'

(PS, as a psychologist, I am proud to say I know my shit – phew!)

Being full of shit

Being full of it means you don't know jack shit – or that you are a braggart and a blowhard.

You mightn't know *you're* full of shit until someone has the guts to tell you, but you probably know lots of other people who are full of it.

If someone is full of shit, you might politely tell

them so in a subtle way (with a smiley face and good body language), 'You're full of shit,' or you might just walk away.

If someone tells *you* you're full of shit, try and suck in the angst and give it a bit of thought. It might be interesting to ask them for their evidence as to why you are full of it. They might give you honest feedback, or they might be full of it themselves, in which case you can ignore them.

Sometimes you can be full of shit just for fun – otherwise called joking around; then, if someone says, 'You're full of shit' and laughs, then you're a funny guy/gal.

Bullshit (also known as horseshit) or bull for short

Bullshit can be good-natured banter or rubbish talk (inaccurate, pretentious or foolish). Both these are covered in full of shit.

Bullshit is a bit like the word bastard. In Australia, a bastard can be a good mate – as in 'Ya stupid old bastard, here have a tinny' (a can of beer).

Or they can be a despicable person, as in 'You bloody mongrel bastard. I'll punch yer head in.'

Good bullshit could be countered with, 'Your talking bullshit, ya silly bastard – here have a tinny' or if it's bad, 'that's bullshit. I'll punch yer head in ya bastard!'

Bullshit is not all bad. Like 'full of shit' – it can be fun, depending on the circumstances.

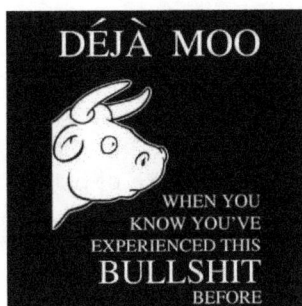

DÉJÀ MOO

WHEN YOU
KNOW YOU'VE
EXPERIENCED THIS
BULLSHIT
BEFORE

Bullshit meter

We all have one of these. We know when we're being spun a yarn, having the wool pulled over our eyes.

Trust your bullshit meter. It's connected to your intuition, which is usually trustworthy and will 'steer' you right (no, I am not sorry for the – pun - although if you were pedantic, you would know that a steer and a bull cannot be the same creature).

Being scared shitless (or shit scared)

Fear is mostly not real; that is, it's out of proportion to the actual threat. Try not to overreact with fear. For example:

Unreal things that scare us shitless (try not to be so over-reactive to these)

- People not liking us
- Not being as cool as our friends
- Fronting up to a party when you're shy
- Having to present to a meeting/public speaking
- Losing our partner (being insecure)
- Losing our job (being insecure)
- Being found out for cheating, and don't text!!!

    'Chexting' is my term for 'I'm not *really* cheating. We're just texting – as friends. It's a work thing.').

Oh really? Pardon us if we're just a *little* bit suspicious.

They're all scary, for sure, but they're *not life-threatening*. Remember the P of perspective.

How to cope with being scared shitless over things that aren't real

Most things come into this category. Here's what to do.

- Take a deep breath and get things in perspective
- Practice being scared shitless, but do it anyway!
- Tell yourself, 'If this doesn't work, it won't be the end of the world.' You can get up, brush yourself off, and start again.
- Take action or be proactive.

If those suggestions don't work – get help. It is too stressful to go through life being scared shitless over fears that aren't life-threatening.

Things that might *legitimately* scare you shitless (*are* life-threatening) are:

- Watching another car about to hit you when you're driving and *not* being able to do anything about it (this actually happened to me)
- Falling off a ladder
- Being at the Zoo when the tiger does escape (this is not common)
- Having a loved one become sick or die

How to cope with *legitimate* things that might scare you shitless:

- You will have little control (you may shit yourself, literally). BOB doesn't want you to have control because it doesn't want you to think (use your Front of Brain). 'Don't analyse that tiger', BOB says, 'Just get out of the damned way!' Our survival brain is well equipped to cope with real fears. It will make you fight, run away, freeze, or fawn (shrivel or grovel, as in 'Stockholm Syndrome'). We can do some pretty cool shit when we are truly threatened (like lifting a car to get a loved one out from underneath).

- The Vagal Breath is always the first port of call. Breathe down into your tummy and right up into your chest – count to three – let it out *very* slowly and focus on the breath only! And repeat. This will help you not to panic and let you assess the threat and deal accordingly

- Your reaction might be counterintuitive, so keep your head. For example, in a stampede, you might fight against the crowd. Like fighting against a riptide, this can put you in greater danger. Don't react – *respond*. Go with the flow until you can get to safety. Keeping your head when you're panicking is hard. Just do the best you can.

'What on earth would I do if four bears came into my camp? Why I would die, of course. Literally shit myself lifeless.'

— Bill Bryson, A Walk in the Woods: Rediscovering America on the Appalachian Trail

PS – Bears *do* shit in forests.

Losing your shit/going 'ape shit.'

You know you have 'lost your shit' when

- You completely lose your temper and scream at someone/something until they run away or your throat hurts
- You have entirely lost control of the situation
- You have freaked out
- You are punching something or someone

None of these is recommended. Losing your shit goes around in a cycle – you lose it because you are stressed, then when you lose it, you get more stressed. The more stressed you are, the more you lose your shit.

How to cope with losing your shit

Intervene as soon as you become aware that losing your shit is a possibility and take action:

- Take a deep breath and a mental step back – let the breath out slowly. Now *respond*
- Walk away
- Put down the phone/hang up
- Get your shit together and get organised (see earlier)
- Wait until you can lose your shit in a semi-controlled way that doesn't involve your partner, workmates, children or animals, e.g.:

  Use a punching bag (or thrash yourself at the gym)

  Roll up a towel and bash the bed

  Punch the pillow

  Put on loud rock and roll, dance like an ape and sing/scream along

  Chop wood (preferably Mallee roots or some wood that's rock-hard)

  Go to the golf range and hit balls until you drop

If you lose your shit – apologise and accept the consequences (which could be severe).

Most importantly, get your stress bucket down by getting your shit together. You may need professional help in the form of anger management if you continually lose your shit.

Accept that shit (not reacting)

When shit happens, our first instinct is often to react. We:

- Catastrophise about it
- Go up the back of the cave, wait for that shit to go away (see Stress and avoidance coping), or ignore it (denial).
- Get angry about it (see not losing your shit)
- 'Chicken Little' about it (run around in every-diminishing circles exhausting yourself

Don't do any of these things. Accept the thing/person/situation. Acceptance doesn't mean you have to like or approve of it—it just is what it is. Accept it. But then—take action! Make a plan. Never forget, the brain loves a plan (I'll keep saying it). Without it, BOB will start to panic, and you will lose even more shit. Acceptance is not inaction.

> 'Acceptance doesn't mean resignation; it means understanding that something is what it is and that there's got to be a way through it.'
>
> — Michael J. Fox (Smart guy and a personal hero)

Let go of that shit

Do you hang on to your shit way past its use-by date? I'm talking about resentments, grudges, guilt, and anger – historical shit.

I once treated a woman who told me a dramatic story about how she was wronged. 'When did this happen?" I asked. She answered (with gusto), '25 years ago!' For 25 years, she was hanging onto that shit! Was she at peace? Was she happy? No, she was not.

Hanging on to your shit can cause serious issues. You never move on. You're in a state of perpetual shit. Shit has happened, and because you can't let it go, it is still happening today, and you are dragging it around after you like a big blob of shit, like an anchor holding back your big beautiful ship with the silk sails that is about to take you forward into peace and contentment. Get rid of it! You will have the *memory* of the old shit, but hopefully, it will be a distant memory and one you can quite easily let go of with a 'Well, that was then, and now is now!'

How to let go of old shit

- Get that old shit together (write it down/make a list of what you want to let go of)
- Consider what impact it's having on our life now and how it's affecting you and your relationships.
- Be determined to let it go. Are you ready?
- Accept what happened (this does not mean approval – see Accept that shit)
- Accept the bad feelings. It was shitty. It was OK to feel bad about it, but it's time to move on
- Try to let go of being a victim. Take up your power now, in the present

An exercise in letting go of old shit

Close your eyes and take five deep breaths. Now, imagine all your shit like a big blob of black stuff on the bottom of the ocean of your life. Between it and your beautiful ship are big stringy black ropes of shit. Imagine an implement to cut off those ropes so your ship can sail. Think a knife, a gorgeous pair of golden scissors, a chainsaw, a wrecking ball—whatever suits you. Keep hacking away at those ropes until you're free.

Think about all the beautiful stuff in your ship that you're taking into your new way of life. What is in the hold? Peace, contentment with occasional spikes of happiness, success.

Also, even though you might find it hard, see if you can practice forgiveness towards whoever wronged you.

Let them go. After all, chances are they're not giving a shit about you. More than likely, they've moved on long ago, and if they haven't – don't give them the satisfaction of holding back your ship. Don't give a shit.

How to let go of new shit (that just happened)

That piece of shit just said a shitty thing that is making you lose your shit. Don't do it! Let it go! Take a deep Vagal Breath, then mentally take a step back and let that shit go through to the keeper. Then *respond*. Revenge is not the only dish best served cold (or at least calm). Be assertive!

I reiterate – if the shit is a real tiger about to jump on you – fight or run like hell – sometimes BOB is right!

You feel like a piece of shit – (not worthwhile)

This can mean you feel off-colour or sick, but sadly, many people think that they are not worth jack shit/not worthwhile. They are not confident and have low self-esteem.

They buy this shitty story because of, for example:

- Their personality
- Bullying at school
- Being abused
- Being poorly parented
- Having a shitty partner or boss who constantly invalidates them

This is serious shit.

People who buy the 'I am not worth jack shit' story have all kinds of problems, up to and including self-harm and suicide.

Do not buy this shit. It has been put upon you by others (and yes, maybe by you—but not all of you—

just a part of your brain that is not quite functioning as well as it could).

You can change it—believe that.

How to cope with feeling like you are not worth jack shit

- Have realistic expectations of yourself. You don't have to be perfect all the time or even feel great about yourself all the time. You are OK most of the time, just the way you are. If you think others have a problem with this, that is their shit and not yours

- Feel sorry for yourself, but in a kind, empathetic way. Talk to yourself nicely, and encourage yourself. Physically stroke and pat yourself (maybe not in public)

- Find things to be grateful for. It could always be worse. Think about those in worse shit than you. Send them good thoughts or volunteer to help them

- Try to be around people who support you and don't make you feel like shit (you can tackle those shits later when you feel better about yourself)

If all else fails, get help.

When you look like shit

We all want to look good. No one wants to look like shit. If you don't care whether you look OK or not and don't look after your appearance, it can be a contributing factor to being diagnosed with a mental illness (it's one of the things we assess). It's human nature to want to look good (pre-historic humans dressed themselves up with shells, paint, and feathers).

You can look like shit because:

- You've been overdoing it (parties, alcohol, work, stress)

- You're ill
- You *think* you look like shit because you're not perfect (overweight/not classically beautiful/have lousy hair, teeth or nails.)
- You're not getting enough sleep, exercise, or nutrition.
- You aren't caring for yourself (lack of time/ energy/motivation)

Not caring about what you look like and not doing anything about it, even though you look like shit, could be a sign of emotional unwellness (for example, anxiety/depression). Get help, or else you could end up in deeper shit.

> Drum: *'Ouiser, you look like hammered shit'.*
>
> Ouiser Boudreaux: *'Don't you talk to me like that!'*
>
> Drum: *'Oh, I'm sorry, you look like regular shit'.*
>
> — Ouiser and Drum from 'Steel Magnolias'

What to do when you look like shit

Whether or not there's a deep underlying emotional or physical unwellness or you looking like shit is due to partying or lack of self-care:

- Give a shit
- Don't catastrophise or fret; accept you look like shit, then:
- Take action to look after yourself better:

    Go for a walk

    Get your hair done

    Have a few alcohol-free days

    Take care dressing for the day

    Eat properly

- Get perspective; you're not perfect; nobody is. Do your best

- Don't compare yourself to others. They have better genes. Get over it and make the best of what you've got

- A psychologist friend of mine once said, 'Life's short; wear your party pants.'

Vain trifles as they seem, clothes have, they say, more important offices than merely to keep us warm. They change our view of the world and the world's view of us. There is much to support the view that it is clothes that wear us and not we them; we may make them take the mould of arm or breast, but they mould our hearts, our brains, our tongues to their liking.

—Virginia Woolf

When you talk shit (Can't communicate)

Not being able to communicate well can cause all kinds of shit:

- Poor relationships

- Fights and misunderstandings

- People manipulate and walk all over you

- It holds you back in your career (unless you're a tech nerd—sorry, tech nerds)

- Dysfunctional self-communication makes you S.A.D (Stressed/Anxious/Depressed) and self-conscious and holds you back in the world and in yourself.

How to communicate better

- Be assertive. Assertiveness is standing up for yourself without hurting anyone or squashing on their rights (it is not being rude, pushy or aggressive). See 'The assertiveness formula' below)

- Learn how to say NO (see the appendix 'How to say NO)

- Listen and focus only on the person you are talking to (if you feel nervous, take deep breaths)
- Watch your body language and tone of voice (be open, speak lowly, slowly and kindly). Also, watch the other person's body language.
- Be brave—give it a go
- Practice, practice, practice!

Do all of the above when talking to *yourself.*

Talk to yourself like you're your own best friend. Be assertive with yourself when your brain gives you rubbish, and let it go. Be:

Self-compassionate

Self-encouraging

Not

Self-critical

Self-judgemental

See 'How to Communicate With Yourself and Others' in the appendices.

Learn – read, research, get help. This is one of the most essential skills you will ever learn.
Communicating is one of the two ways we bond with people (the other is touch, and sometimes you just don't want to go there).

The assertiveness formula

This is handy in a shitty situation. There are four steps.

Step 1: Say 'I have a problem' (state the problem, e.g., 'I don't like the way you speak to me.'

Step 2: Say how it makes you feel, e.g., 'It makes me feel worthless' (or sad, invalidated, angry, or whatever it makes you feel.

Step 3: I think I know how you feel (this is empathy; it shows you've tried to see their point of view). For example, 'I think you feel angry that

I disagree with you.'

Step 4: 'But I would prefer,' e.g., 'I'd prefer it if you let me have my point of view and didn't judge.' *Never begin until you've decided what you would prefer.*

How I learned not to be nervous about talking to people on radio and television

As a cadet journalist, I was offered a job on a country radio station. I was shit scared about being on the radio. Previously, I had been a cadet (zero class) for a country newspaper and could hide behind a font. Now, I would be exposed for the fraud I was in front of thousands and thousands of people. My boss at the time, a beaut bloke called John Hunn, gave me a precious piece of advice. He said:

> *'Muriel, you are not talking to thousands of people all gathered around one radio. Everyone has their own radio. Just talk to one person.'*

What a gem! I was OK from then on and never had a problem.

You can do that shit – self-confidence.

> *'I rise from my seat, awkwardly clutching my handbag and notes to my body. I enter the interview room in a fucked-up-question-mark-posture, walking as though I am ten shits behind.'*

— Danielle Esplin, Give It Back

Can you relate to this? This woman is *not* confident!

To be confident, you need to:

- Have your shit together
- Know your shit
- Know you are not a piece of shit – you're worthwhile
- Don't look like shit

- Be able to communicate

- Remember all the times when you've been confident and succeeded (not the times you've failed). I call these 'Moments of Mastery'. Make a list of yours.

Work on your self-confidence–learn and practise. Take drama and public speaking classes. Self-efficacy and self-confidence are built on past successes. 'But I haven't had any?' you say. Then, visualise yourself being confident. To your unconscious, imagination is as good as the real thing. See yourself standing up there and giving your speech or whatever it is you want to be confident at doing. It's OK to be nervous. Be brave. Do it anyway. Visualise it over and over until you feel less nervous. Fake it till you make it. Act 'as if'. Practise with a friend or family member.

As Aristotle said:

> *'Acting virtuous will make you virtuous.'*
>
> *'Imagination is powerful shit.'*
>
> — Muriel

Don't put shit off (procrastinate)

My favourite theory about procrastination is that it is born out of fear.

You catastrophise so badly about the thing you are *not* doing that BOB (survival brain) sees it as a real and present danger. Therefore, BOB will do everything in its power to make you avoid doing it.

It is avoidance coping.

The fact that this only stresses you out more makes BOB more determined to keep you away from 'the feared stimulus' (psychobabble alert) and round and round the cycle you go.

What to do about procrastinating

Describe the task/situation to yourself in a self-encouraging, kind, and empathetic way. Make sure you talk to yourself about it in a friendly tone of voice (just like you'd say to your best friend).

E.g., 'I know we might be a bit scared of that project, but it's going to be OK, really it is. We can cope—we'll be safe, and all we need to do is take the first step. Take big breaths; open the computer—that's right. See, nothing's happened; see, no tigers. Now, fire it up. Come on, you can do it. Well done! Now, put your hands on the keyboard. See, we're OK. Now make a little start, and then we'll see what happens'.

By now, you might be feeling like a bit of an idiot, but notice how BOB is soothed. You've convinced it that the thing you've been avoiding is not a big, hairy, person-eating beast.

'Just do 10 minutes'

This is my other favourite anti-procrastination method: 'I'll just do 10 minutes' of the project or housework. This can turn into 20 or 30 minutes or even an hour! Sometimes, miraculously, the thing even gets finished!

Get rid of that shit! (De-cluttering)

Hanging on to stuff can be a severe problem. The media has made entertainment out of showing mentally distressed people tunnelling their way through piles of junk. If you are this bad, get help.

If you're just disorganised – here are some ways to cope.

- Get help—get counselling—or there are de-cluttering specialists who will help you sort out your stuff. They will also help you source and organise storage. They cost, but if you can afford it, they're worth it.

- If you're going to do it yourself, start with the good old list. What is important to you that you want to keep? If it's that important, then keep that shit! It might be photographs, mementos, family heirlooms or stuff you've collected (collectibles are much easier to organise and enjoy if you store them properly). If it's on the 'Doesn't mean much to me' list – then chuck it.

- Get in those cupboards and pantries and throw out every bit of shit that you have not used for the last few months. Be ruthless (if you can't, and you absolutely *must* keep that spice that was past its use-by date in the year 2000 or the butt ugly gravy boat that was handed down from Auntie Mavis that you hate but think you *should* keep— you might need to get help!)

- Do a little bit every day (just do 10 minutes).

- Take it to the charity shop. Share that shit! See— that wasn't too hard.

- Do the 'Oprah Winfrey' trick (I believe she started it). Hang or store everything in your wardrobe/closets the wrong way around, then when you use it, put it back the right way around. After six months, chuck out everything that's still the wrong way around (unless it's a family heirloom).

- Call a friend. Doing it with someone else is better.

- Get empty boxes, label them 'Rubbish,' 'Charity shop,' 'Keep & store properly,' and, when they're complete, ' fulfil your promise to yourself and follow through.

Cleaning out your shit is a very healthy thing to do, so do it!

'The best way to choose what to keep and what to throw away is to take each item in one's hand and

ask: "Does this spark joy?' If it does, keep it.

— Marie Kondo. Although she changed her mind about the amount of stuff you can have, this is still a good way to sort out junk.

A piece of shit/a heap of shit and what to do when it is

It's a lemon.

You know when you've bought a piece of shit. It doesn't work, let alone live up to your expectations. Be an assertive consumer and take that shit back. Not doing so just makes it harder for other consumers. It's hard, it's embarrassing, but front up. Be polite and ask for a refund or an exchange. If they won't give you one and you call Consumer Affairs, they could be in the shit.

Your work is a piece of shit

You know when you've done a piece of shit. You can see it on the Boss's/customer's face even before they complain. They're not happy. You can try and bullshit, but if you know that it's a piece of shit, 'fess up and fix it. It's the right thing to do. They might be a shit and be too demanding (your work might *not* be a piece of shit at all), but I'm talking about when *you* know it's a piece of shit.

If you know it's a piece of shit, and you try to bullshit your way out of it, well, you're being a shit, and your values might need a makeover. If it's not a piece of shit, but the Boss/customer is a shit – then be assertive and put your case, or you might decide to make a strategic withdrawal if it's turning into a shit fight. Is it worth it? It's up to you.

You're a piece of shit!

This insult has caused many a shit fight. Make sure you mean it.

True story: From next door's roof, two Myna birds were eyeing a small plastic bag left on our outside table. After a lot of deliberating, they flew down, pinched it, and hauled it back up on the roof. They pecked at it furiously, only to discover that it was dog shit (courtesy of the now sadly late Wilbur the Schnoodle).

In high dudgeon, they picked it up, flew down and threw it back on our outdoor table in disgust. 'Here', they said, 'you can have that shit back!'

> *Life's a piece of shit,*
> *When you look at it,*
> *Life's a laugh, and death's a joke, it's true*
> *You'll see it's all a show*
> *Keep 'em laughin' as you go*
> *Just remember that the last laugh is on you*
> *Ohhhh*
> *Always look on the bright side of life*
>   — Excerpt from Monty Python's 'Life of Brian'

How to know when someone is shitting you

They're lying – It's a crock of shit

Someone is shitting you not only when they are annoying you (when they are being a shit or giving you the shits) but when they are *lying* to you, putting one over you – pulling the wool over your eyes.

Here are the most obvious signs:

- Their tone of voice goes up, and they start talking fast
- They won't make eye contact
- They blush
- They bite their mouth
- They put their hand over their mouth
- Their body language, in general, doesn't match up with what they are saying

• Their smile doesn't reach their eyes

If they are shitting you well enough that you fall for it, that's life. As soon as you realise they are shitting you—take action.

Alert! Some people are extremely good liars. They're on the sociopathic spectrum, or they actually believe their own lies (pathological liars), or they're just bloody good at it! If you get sucked in by one of the above, don't beat yourself up.

I once worked with a pathological liar. Yep, sucked right in—and nearly sued for the bad instructions they gave me!

'You're shitting me.'

This can either be an exclamation of disgust, as in, 'You can't pay me back the money you owe me? – you've got to be shitting me!'

Or good humour, as in 'Climbed Mount Everest without oxygen? You've got to be shitting me!'

Note—I just spelled 'shitting' wrong and have discovered after all this time that my spell checker will not correct shit or any variation of it. This needs to be addressed.

When you're dropped in the shit/been shat on from a great height

Betrayed, told on, dobbed in

You weren't told, you're unprepared, you walk into the meeting, only to be jumped on and have the shit kicked out of you. Don't panic (see 'When you're in the shit').

Being dropped in it is bad enough, but when a trusted family member, friend, or colleague drops you in it, that's got to hurt! Some relationships never recover from this. This is especially hurtful when you didn't do anything wrong (or at least mean to). You are the butt of a cruel joke, the object of a narcissist's pleasure or the 'patsy' designed to take the blame.

You have been shat on from a great height, and any protestations on your part might only make you look guilty (*'The lady dost protest too much, methinks'*— Shakespeare) or stupid.

I have been in this position, and it was one of the most excruciating moments of my life and so stressful I can feel BOB start to fire up just thinking about it.

How to recover (from being dropped in the shit)

- Immediately control the panic with deep Vagal breaths and mentally step back (don't forget to let the breath out – *slowly*)

- Control emotion/distress with the same breathing technique

- Make an immediate, tactical withdrawal to think and plan your next move. If you say anything now, it will probably be what you wish you *hadn't* said when you think about it later

- Call a trusted friend/family member/colleague/ mentor (or two)

- Make your first move. In my case, it was to call an Industrial Relations lawyer)

- Decide on your plan of action

- Stick with people you know you can trust

- Be prepared for grief and loss (loss of trust, status, position, job, person, relationship)

- Stand up for yourself in an assertive way (not passive or aggressive), and if you don't feel like you can do this, get someone to do it for you (or get help)

- Try not to let it make you lose faith in people or be pessimistic. It will pass!

- Don't let it turn you into a victim

If you're genuinely in the wrong and you got found out, well, stiff shit. They got you fair and square, but 'all of the above' still applies.

People treat me like shit

Why are they treating you like shit?

Are they prejudiced, discriminating against you or bullying you?

Are you *allowing* them to treat you like shit? That is not being assertive and sticking up for your rights. If this is the case, learn assertiveness (see the assertiveness formula earlier, 'How to Communicate With Yourself and Others' and 'Assertive Communication' in the appendices). It helps with your confidence in your ability to handle difficult people.

These are all interesting fact-finding questions because once you *know* why people are treating you like shit, you can take action and do something about it.

If they are treating you like shit because there's something about you that is genuinely not acceptable, then take it on the chin and do your best to change it (e.g., be nicer, less grumpy, and easier to get on with).

If, on the other hand, it's because they *are* discriminatory, prejudiced, or a bully, then you can take civil action against them. Contact Legal Aid, Human Resources, or your union, or get advice.

If they are plain mean, you still have recourse. Bullies should not be allowed to get away with their behaviour. Tell someone, get support.

Ultimately, if all else fails, you may need to make a difficult decision about removing yourself from people who treat you badly—even your own family, at least for a while.

Miscellaneous shit

Here's some light relief.

If you're in major shit, you can come back to this bit and skip to 'How to cope with major shit.'

'Stiff shit'/Tough shit.'

In other words, 'If you don't like it, too bad' (it's not/is no longer my problem).

This is one of life's great questions; 'Whose problem is it?' If it's not your problem, don't apologise and don't make it your problem; it's theirs and theirs alone. Tough shit!

Shit for brains

This can be castigation, 'What have you got? Shit for brains!', or a description, 'They've got shit for brains,' and it can be about a one-off incident or about that person in general, as in 'There goes shit-for-brains.'

Chickenshit

A coward, a contemptible person. A dastardly, craven poltroon. Also, a useless thing. 'That car's chickenshit'.

"I may not know much, but I do know the difference between chicken shit and chicken salad."

— US President Lyndon B. Johnson.

Batshit

The situation is crazed, angry or hyper. Also, weird, wonderful, crazy. 'It was batshit, man," could be fantastic or chaotic. Do not tell someone who is batshit to calm down today, or, at the very least, you will get a verbal slap, especially if it is a woman. Women have been called batshit and institutionalised merely for standing up for themselves, as told in Leah Shelton's stunning performance creation 'BATSHIT'.

Dipshit/Shitwit

A person who has shit for brains could also be described as a dipshit or shitwit – a stupid or incompetent person. 'How was the job today?' 'Shitty – they're all dipshits. Except for me, of course.'

Hot shit versus cool shit (Love that shit!)

Hot shit is exciting and, well, hot! (As in, 'Wow, man, that shirt is shit hot').

Cool shit is just, well, cool (as in, 'That's some cool shit you've got going on there').

Either way, this is good shit.

You're the shit

It is a compliment towards someone. It roughly translates to, 'You are the coolest.' (Urban Dictionary)

Good shit vs bad shit

Good shit is, well, good, as in 'this is good shit' or 'this is the shit'. This can refer to music, fashion, food or any experience you're loving. Be careful what you describe as 'good shit' since this can refer to drugs, especially cannabis.

Bad shit is, well, just shitty.

Ratshit

See 'It's a piece of shit'. It is useless—substandard. You paid for it, and you wish you hadn't because they won't give you a refund. Caveat emptor (buyer beware).

Pushing shit uphill

Life is a struggle; you have nothing left in the tank, everything has turned to shit, and life is a shit show.

You have had it. You're not doing it!

I'm not pushing shit uphill with a rake in the pouring rain!

— Drew Broberg—truck driver

Happy as a pig in shit

When life truly is good, you may get to say you're 'happy as a pig in shit' and that's good shit.

Shitkicker

A term for an oaf, an undereducated person, a yobbo, ocker, or bogan who usually takes or is given menial jobs. Be careful with this one; it might, at the very least, be politically incorrect.

'Your father had the shitkicker blues.
Loving you has made me bananas.'

— Guy Marks

Getting shit-faced

You are drunk, plastered, tanked. Maybe you haven't been there (good for you), but this is something you want to avoid if at all possible. You say things that horrify you the next day (if you can remember them). You've come on to your best friend's girl/boyfriend, or you end up chained to a lamp post.

'In vino veritas' means 'in wine there is truth.'

— It's an old Latin saying.

'I don't need this shit.'

What we say when shit happens. Nobody needs shit (unless you really do have a digestive problem, in which case get it fixed; it's as essential as a good night's sleep).

'Everything I touch turns to shit.'

There are times like these. We can't do anything right. For whatever reason, it all turns to shit. Be patient, shit never lasts forever.

'This shit never ends.'

This is a catastrophising statement to the effect that your life will always be full of shit. This is not true. Be more optimistic; everything passes; everything ends; everything is temporary.' 'This too shall pass,' even if it's like a kidney stone.

'This too shall pass' originated in the writings of the Persian Sufi poets. In medieval times, a king brought together wise men to create a saying that would make him happy when he was sad.

They came up with 'This too shall pass.' He was so happy with the saying that he had it inscribed on a ring (so the story goes).

'Holy Shit!'

Where did that come from!? What the...!? You have been surprised and not happily. Or you are unbelievably excited.

You can roll it/a turd in glitter, but it's still shit/a turd

You just can't tart up some things, no matter how hard you try. But don't let that stop you from trying. It's worth having a go. However, if people have a good bullshit meter, be prepared for the consequences.'

They know shit/jack shit/are jack shit

I don't know who Jack is, but he knows nothing and is worth nothing. The origin of the saying is naval—a seaman who doesn't know his jacks (signal flags) from his sheets (sails).

Deadshit

'You're a deadshit mate': you have no idea. You are so stupid it's inexplicable.

'It's deadshit': the situation is unsolvable, irredeemable, it's over.

Bored shitless

The movie, party, or meeting is a dud. You are uninterested and not having fun and wish to be anywhere else doing something even remotely interesting. It's time to bail.

They're a shit-stirrer

We all know them. They're the shit who stirs up trouble just because they can. They often walk away from it once they've had fun. Don't feed shit stirrers by falling for their tricks. Don't react—walk away from the shit.

How to fall in a bucket of shit and come out smelling like a rose

The keyword here is dignity. Dignity is an attitude that is primarily expressed through body language. So, when the shit hits the fan, pull yourself up to your full height, chin up, and hold your head up high. Gesture dramatically and exit stage left (you can fall apart in the wings where nobody can see you). Seriously, body language affects you just as much (if not more so) than others. Shrivelling and grovelling make others wince and make you feel like shit.

No shit Sherlock!'

An exclamation to illustrate that, yet again, someone has pointed out the obvious. This can be a one-off or an irritating habit (in which case, if this is someone you're going to be spending a lot of time with, have the brave conversation and ask them to try not doing it).

'The world has gone to shit.'

Ahhh – it's easy to be cynical about the world today. Turn on any kind of media, and there is the whole, shocking truth. In fact, a lot about the world has always been shit; we just didn't have the all-pervasive, ever-present media to keep shoving it down our throats. Try to avoid the temptation to be cynical. As Max Ehrmann says in his fabulous 1920's poem, 'Desiderata',

> *'The world is full of trickery, but let this not blind you to what virtue there is; many persons strive for high ideals, and everywhere life is full of heroism.'*

I recommend keeping a copy by your bed and reading it often. It is the best piece of advice on life I have ever found. (A copy is in the appendices.)

Enshittification
– Macquarie Dictionary's word of the year 2024

Warning – the last non-politically correct curse word is (almost) coming up.

Noun: The phenomenon of online platforms gradually degrading the quality of their services, often by promoting advertisements and sponsored content to increase profits.

It can also be used to describe the state of the world as described in Jarvis Cocker's song *'C*nts Are Still Running the World.'* Check it out—it's the shit.

As rare as rocking horse shit

This speaks for itself. When you find something beautiful that is this rare, cherish and nourish it.

'Shit a brick'

This usually has an exclamation mark after it. Shit a brick! This is an exclamation of absolute amazement, fear, or anger. This is a good one for almost any occasion when you are thunderstruck.

Shit a brick and build a house

Shock, awe or amazement. There are so many shits you could literally build a structure out of them.

'Shit a brick, lay a stone and fart a crowbar.'
— Kathleen Lily Clare Macarthur (Melbourne radio legend Gary Mac's mum)

Shitting bricks

You are scared shitless, the shit has hit the fan – you've been caught out.

Eat shit and die (also 'Eat my shit')

Something you say to a despicable person.

'Drum, Eat shit, and die!'
— Ouiser to Drum in 'Steel Magnolias'.

Shitshow/shitstorm

A chaotic event or situation, often one that turns out badly: The world doesn't need more bitching about the inevitable, unfixable shitshow that is modern air travel.

A person or thing that is a total mess, failure, or disaster: You'll be cursing that contractor for hours while you try to reverse the shitshow under your new tile floor.

A shit shower (shower of shite)

Either a complete shitshow, or you've run out of toilet paper and have to shower to clean yourself (Eww).

'It's a shit shower, and you don't have an umbrella'.
— My fellow crime writer buddy, Robert Gott

Beat the living shit out of someone.

Not recommended unless you want to end up in jail for assault, violence rarely being a solution (unless it's in self-defence, and even then, it's a dubious solution). It's much better (if you can) to run away and fight another day or restrain yourself.

'You dumb shit.'

Anyone who says this to you is not only questioning your intelligence but could be opening themselves up to a legal stoush since they are also questioning almost everything else about you. Best not to say this to anyone; unless it's with humour, as in 'Muriel, how are you going, you dumb old shit'. This person is asking for it; just saying.

'Shit or get off the pot!'

'Put up or shut up' is said to a blowhard, a try-hard, or someone stalling for time.

They think their shit doesn't stink

This refers to a snob, a conceited, stuck-up and patronising person. Try to avoid these people.

'You must have mistaken me for someone who gives a shit.'

You don't care. You are unimpressed, and this person needs to know it.

The shitter/shithouse

This is the toilet, the outhouse, or the head in a boat.

It can be where you are when you're in the shit as well, as in, 'We're down the shitter now'.

Also, it can be an adjective, as in 'This is shithouse.'

Shoot the shit

Also, 'shoot the breeze'. Have a chat, a natter, a yarn.

It's been a shit year

Any year from 2019 - 2024 (when the World Health Organisation officially declared Covid over) or any year that's been shitty for you.

You couldn't make this shit up

Things are so bizarre that if you made it the plot for a novel or a movie, people would declare it ridiculous. You can't believe it yourself. If it's happening to you, put it in your memoir, then they'll have to believe it.

Dumb as dogshit

This person not only has shit for brains, they show it on a daily basis. Saying this to a person's face could get you in the shit. Putting it in print could get you cancelled or sued (for any number of reasons, not the least of which is that it's dodgy to use the word 'dumb' these days). Whispering it to yourself is OK as long as no one hears you.

Flood the zone with shit

Donald Trump's former chief strategist, Steve Bannon, is said to have started this phrase, which means intentionally flooding the media with misinformation expressly to spread confusion and mistrust. It's arguable that elections have been won with this tactic (one personally repugnant to me). See also 'enshittification'.

A shitpost

A social media term. It's a meaningless post that contributes nothing to the discussion.

New ways to use the word shit happens on a regular basis. It's hard to keep up.

How to cope with major shit

Stress

Stress is not all shit because there is good stress (eustress)—it excites us and keeps us on our toes—and bad stress (dystress). It's the bad shit that does our head in. We owe it to ourselves and to humankind to try and get it under control.

Stress consists of chemicals triggered by the old brain/emotional brain/your paleo brain, which is pre-civilisation. Let's call it BOB (back of brain/the survival brain). Stress is triggered when we're excited, or BOB perceives we are threatened (the second bit is the problem). Our stress bucket overflows into our anxiety and depression buckets.

It's the S.A.D. Cycle.

Here's my depiction of it.

The S.A.D Cycle

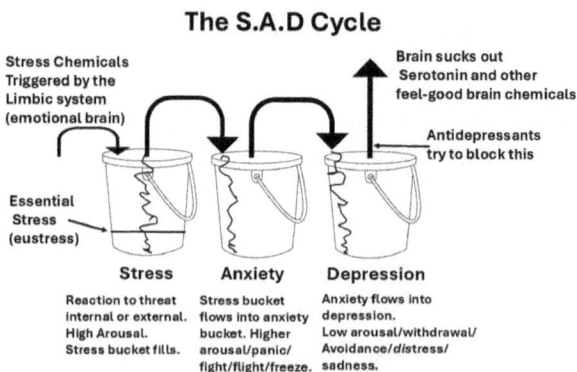

Stress Chemicals Triggered by the Limbic system (emotional brain)

Brain sucks out Serotonin and other feel-good brain chemicals

Antidepressants try to block this

Essential Stress (eustress)

Stress	Anxiety	Depression
Reaction to threat internal or external. High Arousal. Stress bucket fills.	Stress bucket flows into anxiety bucket. Higher arousal/panic/ fight/flight/freeze.	Anxiety flows into depression. Low arousal/withdrawal/ Avoidance/distress/ sadness.

Why does this happen?

BOB wants you to go up the back of some non-existent cave and wait for a non-existent tiger to go away. It has no idea there is no tiger; it just wants you to go to a safe place, curl up in a ball and wait for the tiger to go away or fight that tiger (again, good luck with that one).

Do not let BOB send you up the back of the cave. You might not be able to come out again. If you want to spend some time up there, give yourself permission (have a 'Doona/duvet day'), but make it your *choice*.

Bad stress is extremely corrosive to the brain and body. It makes us cranky (fight or flight) and unwell (because it compromises the immune system, among other things). The brain causes reactions in the body, such as headaches, pains, and feeling seedy. We can get what I call a 'stress hangover' because of the stress chemicals our body has to deal with. Don't worry if you can't remember shit. Stress affects our short-term memory and our ability to think clearly and make decisions.

Knowing your shit about stress can help you to avoid too much dystress.

Knowing about stress

This is especially important because anxiety and depression usually start with stress. A lot of our stress comes from our unconscious. However, one of my heroes, William James, said this about stress.

'The greatest weapon against stress is our ability to choose one thought over another.'

Gautama Buddha said something similar.

'What you think, you become.'

The mind is our ability to be self-aware and to have mindful awareness. It also gives us a greater ability to choose our thoughts. It's located in the middle of the brain on the right-hand side and about halfway back.

This is the seat of willpower, the ability to think about thinking, and the ability to regulate thoughts and emotions. It changes our very body chemistry. It distinguishes us from every other living thing. We need to *use* it!

The mind observes and is aware of the brain, body, and environment. The mind is the watcher; the brain is the organ that thinks, and the body is the engine that feels. Being aware of our mind is mindful awareness/ mindfulness. It's described in my 'Looking, breathing, and letting go meditation' and also in my Simple Brain Training Rules.

What to do about stress

Use your mindful awareness to watch your brain and choose your thoughts carefully. Watch your thoughts and feelings. 'What fires together wires together', so be careful what you fire. The train of thought starts out like a cotton thread, and every time you fire it with intensity, it gets bigger. The thread becomes a cable, then a bicycle tyre, then a car tyre – until it's a huge tractor tyre or even a mining truck tyre.

Don't despair; you can unwire it by practising good mental hygiene and mindful awareness, letting the thought go instead of reacting to it.

It could significantly lower your stress if you choose rational, soothing thoughts over catastrophising, reactive ones.

- See 'When you feel like shit' and 'What to do to feel better.'
- See 'How to get your shit together'
- Do my 'Muriel's looking, breathing and letting go exercise' and practise my 'Simple Brain Training Rules'
- Do my other breathing exercises (also in the appendices)

- Do the visualisation exercises for S.A.D (ditto)
- Don't give a shit when it's not necessary
- Relax. This is a skill – learn it and cultivate it
- Learn how not to worry and ruminate. Do not let the brain get away with rubbish thinking. Be firm with the brain. Gently but firmly tell the thought/s to go away, then re-focus on something else – action and distraction – make tea, go for a walk, think about something else – but do it lickety-split, or the brain will want to pull you back into the worry/rumination
- Love the shit you're in. When you hate it or fear it, BOB goes bananas. Try loving your problems instead. It sounds harder than it actually is. That person who does your head in – love them (a famous guy called Jesus said this). That situation you fear and hate – send it, and the people involved Unconditional Positive Regard (thankyou Mr Carl Rogers), that is, accept them regardless of what they say or do, as humans with human failings and imperfections; but don't forget to:
- Take action! Don't just sit in stress. Have a plan and follow it

The importance of diet in stress management

If you're going through a period of high stress, I don't recommend going on a low-calorie/low-food diet, especially don't cut down on protein and dairy. Your anti-shitty/feel-good neurotransmitter Serotonin is made in your gut, and it's made from tryptophan, which we get from several sources but primarily protein (animal and vegetable).

Ensure you get plenty of protein, preferably some with each meal, and plenty of fibre. The enteric nervous system (your 'gut brain') needs a healthy gut biome to make serotonin, which in turn makes your sleep hormone Melatonin.

If you want to lose weight, by all means, exercise portion control and avoid highly processed foods and easy carbs like sugar, white pasta, bread, and rice (although they might calm you down, they'll affect your gut). Also, watch alcohol.

That's why we rely on a hot milk drink before bed to help us get a good sleep. Milk is high in tryptophan.

'A grumpy gut makes a grumpy person.'

— Muriel

Shower Visualisation for stress (and other shit)

When you have your daily shower, visualise the stress and other shit as shitty dark matter. Imagine the water as a shower of light, washing it all out. See it going down the drain. Keep visualising it going down the drain until it's all gone (or the hot water's run out, whichever is first).

Anxiety/panic and what to do about it

You are starting to lose your shit. It overflows from your stress bucket into your anxiety bucket with some pretty shitty results. Your heart beats faster, you can't breathe, you're in full 'fight or flight' mode, and if BOB hijacks everything away from your rational brain, you might (for example) have a panic attack. BOB wants you to do something *now*.

- Do deep Vagal breaths (a deep breath, then breathe out slowly) that last for at least six seconds. Make the outbreath as slow as you can.

- Take a deep breath, take a mental step back, let it out slowly and let the trigger go.

- Do as many breaths as it takes, focusing only on the breath. Nine, if possible.

- Wait for it to pass. Remember, everything passes. An anxiety attack never lasts as long as the 'flu – thank goodness. Think of it like being dumped by a wave. You don't know which way is up or down, but eventually, the wave deposits you on the beach, a bit bruised and feeling shitty but alive. While you wait, make yourself as comfortable as possible.

- Accept feeling shitty (see, accept that shit)

- Get help. Having other people around makes BOB feel better, especially if they stroke and soothe you. If nobody is there, hug yourself (thereby releasing the lovely feel-good hormone oxytocin). Self-soothing is powerful shit

- Speak encouragingly to yourself, and *don't* catastrophise.

- See 'Stress' (previous pages)

- Do not fret if anxiety comes for no reason. Who knows what shit is going on in your unconscious brain (notice I did not say mind – remember, the mind watches the brain). The anxiety is there – accept that shit – wait for it to pass, and move on.

- If BOB wants you to go up the back of the cave and stay there – *don't!* Agoraphobia (it means 'fear of the marketplace') is hell. You can't go out of your front door. I know it feels shitty but do it! The more you avoid, the stronger BOB gets. Don't let it get on top of you.

Social anxiety

The thought of that party or big social occasion makes you feel shitty, sweaty, and shaky. You would do *anything* to get out of it and probably frequently do. In which case:

- All of the above applies, but when you feel the fear – *do it anyway!* Never let anxiety stop you from doing what you want, being what you want, or going where you want. Accept those shitty feelings. They won't kill you, and remember, *they pass.*

- When you walk into that room full of people (having dragged yourself from the back of the cave), send them all feelings of love and goodwill and *smile* (hence releasing lashings of beta-endorphins).

- Don't worry if you're not a talker; be a good listener instead. Learn good communication skills, especially how to ask the right questions – a good listener is worth a dozen talkers (trust me on this).

- Stick to small groups. You will probably feel more

comfortable. But when something like a wedding comes along – do it! (You know you can. Breathe and smile – breathe and smile). Who knows, you might even have a good time.

- Expose yourself to social situations even if you feel shitty, and practise, practise, practise!

'But she wished she had the guts to go up to him and say hello. Or possibly break his legs, she wasn't sure which.'

— Stieg Larsson, 'The Girl Who Played With Fire'

Depression

You're sad, sad, and sadder. No motivation. You can't sleep. Not interested in sex or food. Don't want to see anyone. You are beating yourself up – feeling guilty. This is genuinely shitty.

This is how I see it. For whatever reason, your stress and anxiety buckets overflow into your depression bucket, or maybe the stress bucket has gone straight there, and you haven't even noticed anxiety. BOB has given up. You are not fighting; you are running away. BOB is so alarmed it shuts you down. You must go up to the back of the cave, curl up into a ball and wait for the tiger to go away. We know there's no tiger, but BOB doesn't.

In the meantime, you will not do anything that requires energy (in case the tiger comes into the cave and you need to fight). You will keep retreating and retreating. Perhaps the ultimate retreat is suicide, in which case, get help! Or the emotional pain or numbness is so bad you want to replace it with physical pain instead and get the urge to self-harm.

Seriously – get help. Drugs might be required if it's bad enough, but studies show they only work for about a third of people. Talking therapy is as good or better. Talk it through, and get strategies.

The best cure is prevention. Learn how to manage your stress, thoughts, and emotions. Then when shit happens – you'll be better able to cope and hopefully not fall into depression.

In the meantime:

Some strategies to deal with depression

(Alert – if you think you're at risk – at all – please call someone, e.g. Lifeline, or see your medical practitioner)

Major depression may only be treatable with medication and professional help—but:

When depression is reactive to what's happening in your life, e.g., shit has happened and continues to happen, then there's a lot you can do about it.

- Deal with stress. Remember, Stress flows over into Anxiety, and Anxiety flows over into Depression (S.A.D). Lowering your stress bucket is essential.

- Talk to someone (it doesn't have to be a professional, but sometimes that's what it takes)

- Get out (in the fresh air; go out with friends; walk). Don't stay up the back of that cave!

- Exercise!! Walk; stretch/do yoga in a chair; dance to 'up' music

- Do your best to get a good night's sleep (see appendices)

- As best as you can, practise thought and emotion management. Be mindful. Watch yourself kindly, and speak kindly to yourself

- Don't get depressed about being depressed. It's OK not to like it, but don't catastrophise about it. Accept it. That doesn't mean you have to like it – it is what it is. But do something about it.

- Make sure you eat well and remember the vitamins B, C, and D—oh, and eat fish – omega-3 fatty acids are good for your brain.

- Make a list of enjoyable things

- Keep a gratitude journal. Studies show it can change your brain

- Hug something: a person, a pet, or yourself

- Meditate/breathe/visualise beautiful things. I know it seems cheesy, but it really is good for you)

- Watch your posture and body language (don't 'shrivel' or hunch up). Expand your chest by lifting up the cleft between your collarbones (the Manubrium). This improves mood and confidence.

- Just get through the next five minutes.

Breathing and visualisation exercises are in the appendices.

Shit at work

Work is a place where major shit happens. Almost everything I've said before or after this can be found in the workplace. This is where you not only earn a living but make some of your most serious connections. Not all those connections will work out. The job doesn't fit you, or you don't fit the job. This is serious shit. What could go wrong?

Your boss is:

- Mean
- A psychopath
- Doesn't know jack shit
- Is just a shit
- A colleague has shit-canned you to the management to get promoted over you or is sexually harassing you. This is tricky shit. On the one hand, you don't want to take this shit, but on the other hand, you need the money.

Usually, it's a good idea to try and work it out before you resign.

Watch out for these four major workplace stressors:

1. **Role value conflict** (your values don't match up with the bosses or the organisation; – e.g. they don't do things ethically, and you do – very stressful)

   Action: You have a decision to make. Can you live with their shitty values? (sorry, they won't change), or do you have to remove yourself and find a better fit?

2. **Role ambiguity**: This isn't what you signed up for. It's nothing like the job description. You don't know what you're doing, and you're *stressed*.

Action: Be assertive and clarify your position if you can. If not, and you can't manage the stress, a decision needs to be made.

3. **Role overload**: That is precisely what it is. You're being overloaded with too much work, doing too much overtime (paid or, even worse, unpaid).

Action: Clarify your hours and position. Evaluate your situation. If you're not coping and it's not worth it – a decision has to be made.

4. **Environmental**: Too hot, too cold, shitty conditions, too much ambient noise or stress.

Action: If the job is good enough in other ways, you might be able to overlook this. If not, a decision has to be made.

The fifth major workplace stressor is that you're being bullied, harassed, or marginalised by bosses or colleagues. This is serious. If all else fails—a decision has to be made. You might need to take it to a higher authority, or you might need to decide to quit and find a better job with better people. See when you're treated like shit.

What to do

What about quitting? 'That's easy for you to say,' you might think. 'I need this job, or I'm in the shit.'

I hear you and quitting needs to be a last resort. First, you want to try to reduce that shit at work by:

- Improving communications with bosses or colleagues

- Taking it up with HR, Workcover, your union, or Fairwork Australia (or a similar organisation that can advocate on your behalf)
- Manage your stress better (particularly in the case of role overload)
- Get clarification about your role (in the case of role ambiguity)
- Get clarification about your legal or ethical position (in the case of role value conflict)

You could also take a look at *you*.

Am I?

- Over-functioning? (putting in too much effort for little reward or appreciation)
- Being a shit (because I'm tired, stressed and frustrated) – see 'Don't be a shit'.
- Am I too scared to leave this shit (beware of the 'What if's?)

    'What if I quit and I don't get another job?'

    'What if I can't pay my mortgage and I lose my house?'

    'What if I have to take a drop in salary or I lose my status?'

The 'what ifs' will get you every time. Remember, for every 'what if?' there's a 'so what?' The world won't end; you won't die. Don't let fear paralyse you into inaction. It takes courage to make a move sometimes. Be brave. It might be uncomfortable (see Accept that shit)—but you can do it.

The risk if you don't take action could be, at the least, being stuck in a job you hate or, at worst, having a stress breakdown, and trust me—you don't want that kind of shit in your life. It is tough to recover from and often takes a long time, so do something. Don't sit in that shit!

Also see: 'When you've been dropped in the shit' and 'People treat me like shit.'

Shit in relationships

Around 51% of relationships fail. Shitty odds, but the stats are real. No one wants to be in the 51%; everyone wants to be in the 49%. So how do you do that? And what do you do when your relationship is heading down the shitter.

Mistake number one is waiting far too long to take action. You know your relationship is going down the toilet, but you wait, hoping it will magically get better. Sorry, but most of the time, it doesn't. We're designed to be pre-civilized, remember? That means we're likely not to couple up until we're in our late teens, which is when women would have started menstruation. Now, kids as young as ten or eleven are having periods, along with a corresponding sex drive. That's enough to scare you shitless. Also, you would have lived from twenty-nine to thirty-five years old. Very few humans made it past that, which is what made them seem amazing to folks back then. Being old was a miracle; now, oldies are just a nuisance. Okay, I know *you* don't think that way, but many people do.

The point is people didn't live long enough or have enough time or energy to break up. You broke up back then because you were killed or you died of disease. This was true right up until the advent of modern medical science, which manages to keep most of us way past what would have been our use-by date.

Preserving relationships cannot be a matter of chance because the odds are against you. It's better to get in early with the relationship counselling ASAP! Better still, even before they move their stuff into your apartment/place, start setting some ground rules and doing regular work on your relationship.

How to head off a shitty breakup

We could all do with a reality check every now and then when it comes to relationships. You were riding along a smoothly paved highway, and it's suddenly turning to shit, leaving you on a corrugated road.

More often than not, the cause is stress. When stress goes up, so can irritability. Whatever the cause, whether it's you or them. Here are my top relationship tips.

What to do when suddenly, everything about them shits you

Suddenly, every little thing your partner does gives you the shits. I could list them here, but you know what they are. Things you used to tolerate or even think were cute now enrage you. Cultivate tolerance for these things. Take a deep breath and step away from your irritability. Do a reckoning of the good things about your relationship instead of focusing on the small, irritating things. You can ask the other person to stop doing the small, irritating things, and they might try, but old habits are hard to change. You need to have patience, remembering that it can take up to 8 weeks to change behaviour. Try to see the funny side. Picking your nose can seem hilarious when seen in the right light.

If it's a huge issue, stop stewing over it; raise it and try to work through it. Get help if you need to. Exercise tolerance and pick your battles. Irritability is a sure sign of stress in a person or a relationship. Address your issues and practice good stress management.

You haven't learned how to fight

Fighting is shitty, and unless you've done a course in dispute resolution, you're probably still using guerrilla tactics learned in the playground or the backyard. For example:

- Fighting to win instead of resolving the problem
- Listening for ammunition instead of a rational response
- Reacting in order to hurt the other person rather than responding
- Historicalising or futurising and not staying with the present problem
- Bouncing from one problem to another instead of trying to solve the problem that started it all
- Keeping score of all the other's perceived slights and going over and over them in your head ... then arguing about them
- Use good communication with yourself and others
- Use assertiveness (*not* aggressiveness) since 'losing it' often means losing the fight.
- Use good body language: stand tall or sit openly, facing the person, hands at your side. Look the other person in the eye. Don't use threatening body or facial gestures (closed fist, snarling face, yelling). Lower your tone of voice, and speak slowly and strongly
- Negotiate for what you want, don't demand. Tell the other person what you'd prefer – that is, what you'd rather have – instead of what is happening now.

Not thinking as a couple

It's easy to stop feeling like a couple when you're both working and being independent. Also, when only one is working, and the other is not doing paid work, it's easy to lose sight of 'team us'. Inequalities in relationships bring resentment. Women are left behind in their jobs and careers. The facts don't lie; women still do around 75% of the unpaid work in relationships. 'Team us' means working together, and that includes the cooking and chores.

Even if your partner has handed over a chore or a responsibility to you, make sure you include them in decisions about it. Communicate about your relationship regularly and ensure you're both truly happy with the division of labour. Make shared decisions.

Neglecting your friendship relationship

We might start a relationship in the throes of passion, but without a friendship relationship, that passion fades, and the relationship fades, too. There are all kinds of reasons why we're attracted to our partner. Just look at how our mums and dads fit together. Many of the attractions are also unconscious motivations, and we could spend forever trying to work those out. So we need to consciously nurture our relationship with our partner, especially our friendship relationship.

We stop 'hanging out', we don't do fun things together, and we stop catching up with other friends for a drink and a bite the way we used to. Suddenly, our relationship is all about chores. Then, when it comes to sex, that's another chore.

Regain your friendship relationship. Make sure you spend time 'hanging out'. Chat about what's new. Make sure you have at least one thing in common and can have a conversation about it. If you've lost your partner as your best friend, do things to rekindle the friendship. Maybe you've had a good friend who sometimes does some irritating things, but you stick with them through thick and thin. Apply that to your partner.

Trust and intimacy are low

Trust and intimacy are essential to each other and to a relationship. That's not just intercourse. Many people mistake intercourse for intimacy when it's often just sex. Trust is not just about being faithful and responsible; it's about being able to trust your partner with your thoughts and feelings and not have them used against you. When you don't trust your partner implicitly, then sex loses its spontaneity and joy.

I always say sex starts at breakfast – small touches, loving words, holding hands, terms of endearment and affection. Without them, sex is sometimes just going through the motions. For some, it can be a way of avoiding facing up to the problem that you don't *desire* each other anymore; you just want sex. Really good sex means feeling safe; if you don't trust your partner, how can you feel safe?

Trust and intimacy can be nurtured by improving communication skills, regularly sharing thoughts and feelings, and making shared decisions. Sexual intimacy does not necessarily include intercourse and relies on loving touch and mutual satisfaction; however, this is achieved.

R.E.S.P.E.C.T.

Aretha Franklin, the queen of soul, got it right when she sang, 'R.E.S.P.E.C.T.—find out what it means to me.' If you've lost it, it might be hard to regain it, but, along with tolerance, it's essential to a relationship.

Respect is lost when there's a breach of trust. Or someone isn't pulling their weight. You know when you've lost respect for your partner because it brings up a really shitty feeling, ***contempt***.

Be honest. Talk to yourself and/or your partner

about why respect has been lost. If it's you ... choose to change in order to regain respect. If it's them ... ask them to change.

Stay attracted to each other

If you look at your partner sometimes and don't feel attracted to them, that's pretty normal. But if you *never* find them attractive anymore, that's a problem. 'They look like shit.'

Attractiveness might seem superficial, especially if one or the other is ill, but otherwise, attraction is part of what brought you together, and it's important. 'They've let themselves go,' a friend of mine says sadly, meaning their partner no longer makes an effort with their appearance or demeanour. That might be because they're mentally or physically ill, but it might also mean they take their partner for granted or they just don't care that much.

Attractiveness matters. It's not everything, but it's important. If you think it *shouldn't* be, that we should give each other unconditional love, that might be true if you're talking about brotherly love. But if you're talking about intimate relationships, that's entirely different.

If you're not attracted to each other anymore, ask yourself honestly, why? Then, if you are able to change, then try. It might mean a makeover, not just physically but behaviourally and attitudinally. Make an effort. Have regular date nights and dress up!

That's not everything there is to know about relationships, but it's a good start. If you feel your relationship needs more than first aid and it's time for CPR, then you might want to get professional help. If all is lost, consider separation counselling; it will help you get through spitting up. I genuinely hope that's not necessary.

Muriel's 3 Cs of relationships

Communication *Both verbal and non-verbal, it is number one!*

Commitment *No commitment = bad/no relationship*

Care *If the 'care factor' is missing, you're in trouble.*

How to rescue a deadshit relationship

So, you waited too long, and now your relationship is up shit creek. You might not be living with a shit, but the relationship is shitty. This is far too stressful. It's never too late to take action.

If you *are* living with a shit, even if they don't mean to be, then like a shitty job, action needs to be taken. Shitty as it is, the cost of inaction in a bad relationship can be life-threatening in terms of your health, physical, emotional and mental.

See a relationship counsellor/therapist. They are experts at this. Don't be shy. Once you get together in that room, a good therapist will guide you through it until you either break up or get back together.

Even if you don't think you're going to make it, get therapy anyway. Separation Counselling can make the process less stressful. Who knows, you might remain friends.

Re-romanticise the relationship. This is something you needed to do leading up to this crisis. You can try mouth-to-mouth, but if your relationship needs CPR, you're not likely to be feeling very romantic. Try communicating first and get help from a professional if necessary. Then, make sure you have a regular date night when you're back on track.

See most of the rest of this book for other actions you can take.

Parenting shit

I left this till the end because not everyone is a parent.

Parenting can be a shit job. The upside is obvious but it's not always happening. The worst times, most would agree, are the '2 T's of Parenting)

Terrible 2s, and

Teenagers

Two-year-old tantrums are not that different from teenage ones, and the cause is the same – they just want to get their own way and be a person in their own right.

Classical conditioning says that to get a behavioural result, you must pay attention to what (behaviour) you want and ignore what you don't want. However, that can be negative with real children. Treating children like unwanted things (or pets, for that matter) is tragic. Children need to be paid attention to and crucially, they need to be shown love and affection.

If you ignore bad behaviour, that can happen often. Lack of attention can become neglect, and children can act out and become insecure.

Don't ignore them or react against them. Give them firm boundaries and consequences if they break them – and be consistent!

Here are some hints for making parenting less shitty.

Parenting young children

Get close to your child

Getting close to your child lets them know you mean it and makes them more likely to pay attention. Common stumbling blocks can be yelling instructions from a distance, from the other side of the room, from another room, or even across a park.

Bend down to their level and lower your voice. This lets your child know that you mean business and makes it more likely that they will pay attention. It also means that they won't be intimidated by being disciplined.

Be clear and specific

Tell your child exactly what you would like them to do instead of what they are doing. Common mistakes include using vague terms or giving the child too many options. Be very specific and give them an example of what you want them to do. For example, 'Stop screaming and tell me what you would like.'

If they still don't do it, let them know what will happen if they don't, and follow through with consequences, such as taking away a privilege or having quiet time.

If it's important, don't give the child a choice.

If an instruction is critical, phrase it as a direct request rather than a question. Come and have your bath now, rather than Would you like your bath now?

Notice the good things

Let your kids know when they do something you like. Use lots of different ways to show them. Give them a cuddle. Say, 'Well done,' or 'That's great.' For example, 'I really like the way you're sharing.'

Actively look for positive ways to let your child know what you expect. When they're playing well, when they do something difficult, when they try something new, when they help you, or when they show they're worried about another child, these are all positive ways that you can let your child know what you expect from them.

A stumbling block here is forgetting to point out the good things. It's important to make sure there are plenty of positives and that you have fun too, rather than feeling that you're saying no all the time.

Sleep Time

There are two main approaches to getting your child to stay in bed and go to sleep. The first is where a parent stays in the child's bedroom and gradually leaves. The second is to leave the room and, whenever they come out of the bedroom, take the child back.

The key to both is not interacting with the child. Stick to your guns. Children will intensify their attempts to get your attention. The behaviour will get worse, but the strategies will work if you persevere. Research shows that both are equally effective, although the gradual withdrawal of a parent may cause less upset for a young child in the short term.

Time out or quiet time (naughty chairs or naughty rooms)

The key to strategies such as these is that children find quiet time boring rather than punishing. These techniques work on the principle of removing sources of entertainment or reinforcement. Quiet time involves keeping a child in one spot until they calm down and stop behaving in the way that you have asked them not to. Time out is the next step if quiet time doesn't work.

The objective of both steps is for the child to stop screaming or making demands. A common stumbling block is bringing a child out if they are still crying or yelling. Don't ask a child to apologise after time out – bring them back to the activity and then look for an opportunity to give some positive feedback when they are behaving appropriately.

Routines

Having set routines makes a big difference. Children get used to the idea that they play at certain times. Things that you can build in include regular times for – for example:

- Meals
- To play with your children
- For them to play with other children
- For different types of activities, such as reading, going to the park, listening to music, and dancing. Importantly, build in time for lots of fun.

Parenting teenagers

First, remember that 'bad' is a subjective word, and what you think is 'bad behaviour' may or may not be. If we're not going to play the 'blame game,' we could try substituting 'bad' with 'irresponsible' or 'unacceptable'.

So, supposing their behaviour is unacceptable or irresponsible, try to remember that it's their job to question your authority at this time. They are still growing and developing, and that includes their brain, which will keep growing and developing until they're about 26. This might be a possible reason why one study showed the average age of children leaving home was 28 (see 'How to parent adult children still living at home' and many other useful articles on my website, The Talking Room).

As a consequence of us not having any 'Rites of Passage' or 'Rituals' for the transition to adulthood, we have invented the 'Teenager', a kind of 'no person's land' where young people, having no template to follow, have made up their own – for better or worse. Also, let's remember the agony of our own 'between years' of raging hormones and pimples. 'It ain't easy' on either side, but being the parent means having the responsibility of guiding your children (as best you can) into adulthood while not 'crowding' them, but giving them enough rules and boundaries to push against so that they can individuate and become independent. Some or all of the following might be helpful.

Tips for this rocky passage

Be a good role model

- It's hypocritical to expect your teen to come home on time and not get drunk if *you* arrive home 'totalled' at 3 am driving the family car. Drink responsibly or take a cab.

- Try not to be reactive and lose your temper, but rather, be assertive.

- Be there for them, consistent, reassuring, loving, and inclusive. Encourage them to invite friends over at any time (with ground rules).

Talk to your Teen like an adult

- If you expect them to behave like one, pay them the courtesy of communicating with them like one.

Set realistic boundaries and involve them in the decision.

- For example, ask them what *they* think is a reasonable time to get home—you might be surprised.

- Or ask them what chores they would like to do. Maybe ones that fit their abilities. For example, if they love shopping, ask them if they'd like to go shopping at the supermarket.

- Growing up means being able to make decisions for ourselves. Even if you think you know better, try to let your teen make the best decision they can and take it seriously – even if you put it up for negotiation.

What are the consequences of unacceptable or irresponsible behaviours?

- Have a pizza and cola meeting and discuss acceptable consequences – these can be written down and displayed somewhere.

- Consequences can include being grounded, no TV for a night, or no internet access.

- If teens give you an 'attitude' or are rude or disrespectful, direct your communication at their behaviour—**not at them as a person**.

- 'I love you as a person, but that behaviour is absolutely unacceptable'.

Give positive feedback for appropriate, responsible behaviours

- Often, parents fall into the trap of nagging teens for not doing 'the right thing' but not giving good feedback when they do (see 'Behaviour modification for parents and teenagers' on my website, The Talking Room).

Pick your battles

Parents often make things hard for themselves by constantly picking on their teens over 'trivial' things.

What is trivial stuff?

- Who they hang out with (unless you know for a fact they're dealing drugs)

- What they wear (unless they're expecting you to pay – this is negotiable)

- What they eat (point out that they are responsible for their own health – you will provide healthy food, but unless it's a family pizza night, they are responsible for funding their own junk food).

What about homework? – trivial or not?

- Far too many screaming rows result from nagging young people about homework. As parents, you are giving them the opportunity to get an education; it's up to them to follow through. It's up to you to turn up on parent-teacher nights to show support.

- Try to make it clear that study is their responsibility, and you will not be nagging them to get it done. If they fail, that is the consequence of their behaviour, and they have to accept the consequences. However, you will be interested in what they are doing, inquiring about how they are going from one adult to another and offering assistance if required.

What about keeping their room clean – trivial or not?

Generally speaking, fighting with your teen over keeping their room clean and tidy is like trying to hold back the tide. Make them aware that their room is their responsibility, and if they want to live in chaos, that's their problem. Nobody else has to see it as long as they keep the door shut and nothing grows in there.

- See The Talking Room 'How to get Teenagers to do chores'

Set time aside to do things with your teens

- Walking with them or driving them are good times to talk 'one-on-one, ' but there are other things you could do together. Find an activity that fits in with their existing interests or suggest something new as an 'adventure' (camping, for example).

Be patient, be honest and give unconditional love to your teens

- If teens are going to be honest with you, they need to be able to trust you with their disclosures. Without realising it, parents can be ridiculing, dismissive or patronising of teens' disclosures. Building trust means being gentle with their information and their feelings, even if they've got themselves in serious trouble. Reacting and getting mad at them isn't going to help, even if you're doing it out of love and concern.

Phew, made it. Under 100 pages. I hope it helped or gave you a laugh. If you didn't find help or find a strategy, see the appendices for more ideas.

Appendices

Desiderata

By Max Ehrmann, written as instructions to himself after the trauma of World War 1:

Go placidly amid the noise and haste,
and remember what peace there may be in silence.
As far as possible without surrender
be on good terms with all persons.
Speak your truth quietly and clearly;
and listen to others,
even the dull and the ignorant;
they too have their story.

Avoid loud and aggressive persons,
they are vexations to the spirit.
If you compare yourself with others,
you may become vain and bitter;
for always there will be greater and lesser persons than yourself.
Enjoy your achievements as well as your plans.

Keep interested in your own career, however humble;
it is a real possession in the changing fortunes of time.
Exercise caution in your business affairs;
for the world is full of trickery.
But let this not blind you to what virtue there is;
many persons strive for high ideals;
and everywhere life is full of heroism.

Be yourself.
Especially, do not feign affection.
Neither be cynical about love;
for in the face of all aridity and disenchantment
it is as perennial as the grass.

Take kindly the counsel of the years,
gracefully surrendering the things of youth.
Nurture strength of spirit to shield you in sudden misfortune.
But do not distress yourself with dark imaginings.
Many fears are born of fatigue and loneliness.
Beyond a wholesome discipline,
be gentle with yourself.

You are a child of the universe,
no less than the trees and the stars;
you have a right to be here.
And whether or not it is clear to you,
no doubt the universe is unfolding as it should.

Therefore be at peace with God,
whatever you conceive Him to be,
and whatever your labors and aspirations,
in the noisy confusion of life keep peace with your soul.

With all its sham, drudgery, and broken dreams,
it is still a beautiful world.
Be cheerful.
Strive to be happy.

— *Max Ehrmann, 1927*

Rules for good communication with yourself (and others)

Don't blame:

Put all the blame on yourself or the other person.

Don't complain:

Nag, whinge to get what you want – be assertive and ask calmly and clearly – towards yourself and others). Numbers 1 & 2 equal self-blame, guilt and beating oneself up – very self-destructive

Don't over-explain:

Going on and on rationalising, *overanalysing* and trying to make sense of things or justify things to yourself – or others. Be brief.

Don't catastrophise:

You make things worse by repeating them in your head – 'Making Mountains out of molehills'. Try DE-catastrophizing, being positive, and being perceptive.

Don't 'alwaysise':

I/they *always* do this. 'neverise' – 'They *never do* anything for me'/'Nothing good *ever* happens for me – or 'generalise' – apply one thing to everything – 'My *whole* life is bad.'

Don't react! R*espond*:

Stop – take a deep breath – take a Mental step back – think – then do or say. Take a moment to let your rational brain rein in your emotional brain so you don't say something you'll regret later. 'Do the Vagal breath/s – then immediately *re-focus* (don't leave a gap, or your brain will drag you back in).

Don't historicalise:

Dragging up over old stuff, *ruminating* – focus on your *preferred* outcome.

Don't crystal ball-gaze/futurise:

Worrying and visualising negative outcomes for the future. Instead, visualise positive outcomes for the future and what you *want* to happen, and visualise the best-case scenario, *not the worst!*

Try to see the positive in all things at all times:

Refocus your brain onto more positive things and trains of thought and visualise them with enthusiasm, intensity, and desire, 'This is what I want'. It's okay to feel bad or sad, but not all the time.

Be self-observant to catch negative talk and self-talk:

Practice Mindfulness and re-focusing on positive thoughts. Don't be judgemental towards others or yourself with 'downing' self-talk ('I'm so stupid') (see 1 & 2).

Don't mind-read, and don't assume:

If you're unclear about something, Clarify it as soon as possible. Don't make up other people's minds for them. Don't assume what they are thinking. Don't take things personally!

Deal with issues as they arise:

Don't stew on them or avoid them. Take action.

Be assertive:

This applies to how you talk to yourself, too—stand up to yourself. Being unassertive is stressful.

The assertive intervention formula (remember – this is for *you* too)

- 'I have a problem' (State the problem calmly and clearly).

- 'It makes me feel' (Always state your feelings, e.g., 'sad', 'disappointed,' angry').

- Use empathy, e.g. 'I realise you get frustrated when' or 'I understand how you feel'.

- 'I would prefer/I want' (No good saying what you don't want if you don't say what you'd rather have)

Also:

- Watch your body language, especially eye gaze (steady and straight) and tone of voice (low and slow)

- Pick your battles – What am I going to stand up to, and what do I let go? 'Don't sweat the small stuff.'

- Take 'time out'. If you're getting 'hot under the collar', ask for time out to 'cool down'. Make a time to return to the issue (even if it's with *yourself*) – 'I'd like to discuss this at ...... today/ tom.'

- Choose a 'default' fall-back position, e.g. 'We need to agree to disagree' or 'Because I choose not to' - or 'I'm sorry you feel that way' ('But I stand by my position/opinion/decision'.)

Repeat this phrase as many times as necessary (stuck record technique).

Practice *self-compassion* – *self*-encouragement and self-empathy.

Be your own best friend.

How To Say No (to unfair requests and demands)

- Be sure where you stand first, i.e., whether you *want* to say yes or no. If you're not sure, say you need time to think it over and let the person know when you will have an answer. Give yourself time to decide.

- Ask for clarification if you don't fully understand what is requested of you.

- Be as brief as possible, i.e., give a legitimate reason for your refusal, but avoid long elaborate explanations and justifications. Such excuses may be used by the other person to argue you out of your 'no.'

- Use the actual word 'no' when declining. 'No' has more power and is less ambiguous than, 'Well… I just don't think so…'

- Make sure your nonverbal gestures mirror your verbal messages. Shake your head when saying 'no.' Often people unknowingly nod their heads and smile when they are attempting to decline or refuse. Make sure your tone of voice is neutral.

- Use the words 'I've decided not to' or 'I won't have time' rather than 'I can't' or 'I shouldn't'. This emphasises that you have made a choice.

- You may have to decline several times before the person 'hears' you. It is not necessary to come up with a new explanation each time; just repeat your 'no' and your original reason for declining.

- If the person persists even after you have repeated

your 'no' several times, use silence (easier on the phone), or change the topic of conversation. You have the right to end the conversation.

- You may want to acknowledge any feelings the other has about your refusal, 'I know this will be a disappointment to you, but I won't be able to...' However, you don't need to say 'I'm sorry' in most situations to apologise for your refusal. Saying 'I'm sorry' tends to compromise your basic right to say 'no'

- Avoid feeling guilty. It is not up to you to solve others' problems or make them happy.

- If you do not want to agree to the person's original request but still desire to help her or him out, offer a compromise: 'I will not be able to babysit the whole afternoon, but I can sit for two hours.'

- You can change your mind and say 'no' to a request you originally said 'yes' to. All the above applies to your change of mind.

Muriel's Simple Brain Training Rules

- **Your brain and your mind are not the same thing.**

  The Mind *observes* the brain. I call this Mindful awareness or the *me* perspective. There will be differing philosophical points of view on this (dualism vs non-dualism and so on), but if you're in the shits, you won't want to deal with them right now. Trust me. Look at your hand and tell it to make a fist – that's a thought and behaviour of *choice* – not the automatic shit our brain usually serves up to us, i.e. 'Where did I leave my glasses?'

- **Remember, 'what fires together wires together'**

  The brain strengthens anything you pay attention to with intensity. It does not care if it is good or bad for you. So, keep an eye on it with your mind. You want to let go of thoughts, feelings and behaviours you don't want. Feel free to have feelings but don't let them cripple you.

- **Build up your mind-muscle**

  Do my mindful looking and breathing meditation (follow my instructions in the book or listen online) and carry that over into your everyday life. Be Mindfully aware to observe your thoughts, feelings, and emotions and use the mind to help you choose/be responsive to what you want to keep (wire) – and what you want to let go of (unwire). You will probably never *forget* your old mental habits, but you will be able to have more control over them. You will also always have the *memory*. Remember, it's only a memory.

• **The brain is designed to worry and be negative.**

When you decide to let go of a negative mental habit, thought, or any other stimulus – if you don't strongly re-focus on something positive, it will go back to worrying.

• **Have plenty of positive things to re-focus on**

Pleasant memories – things to look forward to – happy pictures – good intentions – affirmations, or favourite songs.

• **Have a list of things you like doing (action and distraction).**

Things that you enjoy and make you feel good – e.g., five-minute walks, a cup of tea, getting out in the fresh air and sunshine, calling a friend. 'What can I do to make myself feel better?'

• **Do not get angry at your old mental habits**

BOB (your survival/stress brain) will want you to worry or be anxious. Accept what it's doing and let it go. Otherwise, if you react to it and stress about stress, you'll only get more stressed (vicious cycle).

• **Focused attention is essential.**

Improve your ability to concentrate and be in the present moment. My 'Looking, breathing and letting go' exercise will help. If you can't focus because you have a condition like AHDH, make sure you get help)

Relaxing Exercises

You will find 30 of my recorded meditations, including instructions. Go to my website, 'The Talking Room', and search 'meditations'. The first four are instructions:

Meditations

01 Abdominal breathing

02 Locating the mind

03 Reattributing thoughts and feelings

04 Basic mindfulness meditation

05 Personal (looking and breathing) meditation

06 The relaxation response

07 Body scan for pain tension

08 Progressive muscle relaxation

09 Gratitude exercise

10 For fear and being stuck

11 Fluffy cloud sleep

12 Relaxing for children and parents

13 Rainbow Adventure for Children and Parents

14 Be the fox for relaxation and sleep

15 Happy mini meditations to relax and sleep

16 Turning negative thoughts into positive ones

17 Changing brain chemistry

18 Visualising your best-case scenario

19 Visualising a goal

20 Asking your wise self for change

21 Improving self-confidence

22 Letting go of bad habits

23 Dealing with bad memories

24 Dealing with grief

25 Letting go of someone

26 For relationship stress

27 For codependency

28 Safety and security

29 In a lush rainforest

30 On a tropical beach

Muriel's 'Looking, breathing and letting go' meditation.

This is a rehearsal for letting go of things all day, every day, but doing the exercise is relaxing and produces feel-good chemicals in your brain (GABA and Dopamine – if you're interested, look them up).

- Close your eyes and breathe down into your tummy (abdominal breathing)

- At the same time, look into your eyelids at what you can see *physically*. (it shouldn't mean anything. Otherwise, your imagination is involved, and we don't want that)

- Do not pay attention to whatever wants to take your attention away from looking and breathing—just let it be and let it go. Don't try to block stuff out—your brain will just want to interfere even more. Notice it (whatever it is—a sound, thought, etc.) and let it go. If you like, you can say, 'Let it go' and focus back on looking and breathing—keep that focus!

- Do it for at least five minutes. After two and a half minutes, you might be able to recognise a 'relaxation response' (body feels heavy or light – you feel relaxed)
- Do it twice a day

Progressive Muscle Relaxation

This promotes physical relaxation, especially when you're feeling tense

Breathe in as far as you can – while tightening each muscle group. As you breathe in more, tighten the muscles more – when you can't tighten them anymore or breathe in anymore – let the breath go with a big whoosh! Saying to your muscles – Relaaax! In this order:

- Hands
- Arms
- Shoulders
- Neck
- Scalp
- Face
- Throat
- Chest
- Upper back
- Upper tummy
- Lower Back
- Lower tummy
- Buttocks
- Legs
- Feet – just do the best you can

Breathe in more and more – tighten the muscles in each group more and more until you can't go any further – then let the breathe out – whoosh!! – and flop the muscles – saying to yourself (muscle group, e.g. hands) 'Hands, relax!!'

You can do this throughout your day if you feel tense in a particular area, shoulders and neck.

Breathing exercises for S.A.D. (Stress, Anxiety, and Depression)

The Vagal breath

- Big chest breath; hold for one … two …three, focusing only on the breath and counting. Then, let the breath out very slowly, like a sigh

- Do as many as you need to for heart/chest/ breathing symptoms

Abdominal breathing

- This basic breathing technique is behind every meditation practice. It induces relaxation. It has a physiological effect on us by slowing down our pulse and reducing our heart rate, regulating the Vagus nerve, which governs our nervous system, and releasing endorphins and GABA. Do it as often as you like for as long as you like

- Make yourself comfortable, sitting in a chair with your spine straight or lying on the floor with your eyes closed.

- Place your hands on your midriff with your fingers only just touching. Your goal is to breathe down into your tummy so that your fingers come apart, even just a little. This shows that your breath is going into the right place. Most of us breathe shallowly into our chests, and this is not conducive to relaxation.

- Keep breathing down into your tummy. Make it a natural breath, and don't force it'

- As you breathe out, close the back of your throat

slightly so that your diaphragm needs to work a little bit; 'sigh' out the breath. This is what I call 'restricted breathing.'

- Focus only on your breath. If anything else tries to take your attention away, let it go and focus back on the breath and getting it into the right place.

- Watch the breath from the moment it comes into your body until the moment it goes, and you are ready to take the next breath.

- Keep doing this for as long as you want to. Don't forget to watch out for the relaxation response. Keep breathing into your tummy, breathing, and relaxing.

Breath, step back and let go (for reactivity)

- Take a deep chest breath. Focus on the breath, taking a mental step back from the person/ situation/thing

- Slowly let the breath out

- Repeat, re-focus your attention on something else or walk away

How to Get a Better Night's Sleep

Cease caffeine after lunch, particularly after 5 pm – don't drink alcohol after 8 pm (after 8 too late!)

Don't drink a lot of fluid after 9 pm – don't go to bed on a full stomach!

One Hour before bedtime – turn off all electronic appliances, especially computers and televisions. Their light is primarily blue, and this turns off your sleep hormone, Melatonin. If you must use them, put on a blue light filter (available on most modern devices).

Put on some relaxing music – have a 'potter' about

To potter means to do inconsequential things. 'Get Ready for Bed'.

Read something – a magazine, novel (preferably not a page-turner) or an inspirational book).

Half to three-quarters of an hour before bedtime have a hot milk drink (milk contains tryptophan, a sleep-inducing substance). You can add Milo or raw honey. Also, perhaps an herbal remedy for sleep like Valerian or Melatonin (Circadin is good. You will need to see a GP for this – but don't mix it with sleeping medication).

Other vitamins and supplements that can help with sleep are Vitamin B complex at breakfast or lunch, extra B6 at bed (make sure your daily intake of B6 doesn't exceed 100 mg), Magnesium Complex, Theanine from tea and 5HTP (this is tryptophan which makes Melatonin, your sleep hormone).

Also, clean your teeth and take off your makeup at this time (don't wait till you're sleepy to splash water on your face).

Wait until you are sleepy or drowsy, then go straight to bed. Just being 'tired' is not the same because sleep comes in waves or cycles. It is OK to continue reading your non-arousing material in bed or make a 'reading nook' somewhere close by if other sleepers are involved.

Important – Make light bulbs warm/orange (not blue/cold, as this discourages melatonin).

If you are not asleep within 15 minutes of settling down or you wake in the night, Get up.

Do not lie in bed in the dark staring at the ceiling or tossing and turning – **get up** and read/listen to music/ potter until you are sleepy again. When you go back to bed, close your eyes and breathe in for the count of 3, hold for 3 and out for the count of 3, or do a meditation breathing exercise (breath down into your tummy, breathe out, and on the outbreath say 'one' to yourself). If this does not work – get out of bed and 'potter' some more until you feel sleepy again – then go back to bed

Don't 'Catastrophise' about the fact you are taking time to go to sleep – accept it. Otherwise, you will just stress yourself. If you're awake – you're awake.

Don't have a television or computer in use in your room or use your phone unless it has a blue light filter – bed is for sleeping. Encourage this by saying to yourself when getting into bed, 'Bed is for sleeping' (or cuddling or making love.). Champagne and strawberries are OK on special occasions only.

Keep your bedroom cool, quiet, and dark! – dark encourages Melatonin. This is hugely important.

Have a regular wake-up time – This is more important than a regular sleep time. Open the curtains or go outside as quickly as you can when you wake up. Look into the blue sky to turn off your melatonin, especially if you are depressed or have a fatigue syndrome such as CFS. You don't want your fatigue and your sleep hormones to combine.

Catnaps or powernaps are great, but not after 2 pm and don't nap for more than 25 minutes (or at night, your brain will think you've already slept). Have a timer nearby to wake you up at 20 minutes.

If you are still not sleeping properly after a reasonable period of time, consult your physician. A good night's sleep is essential to your proper mental and physical functioning, and a short course of medication might help you get into a routine.

For worries/intrusive thoughts, use Thought Stopping/mindfulness, relaxing breathing, and visualising. Also, journal/write down worries – and do the gratitude exercise.

Visualisation Exercises for Stress, Anxiety Depression

Emotional memory exercise

Do breathing and looking into your eyelids until you feel more relaxed.

Now, open your inner eye into your imagination and imagine one of the most wonderful things that has ever happened to you, or *could* ever happen to you. Or imagine a time or place where you feel content with the world with no worries; nothing to do – nowhere to go.

Go over it in every minute detail (smell it, feel it, taste it). Smile at the memory of it (or the thought of it. Let the joy and contentment of it flood your whole mind, brain, and body).

Now open your eyes and refocus on something that makes you feel OK (a thing or a thought).

Favourite/safe place visualisation

Do breathing and looking into your eyelids until you feel more relaxed.

Open your inner eye into your imagination and imagine a place where you have absolutely loved being; the beach, mountains, somewhere in the world you love, somewhere with pure joy and no baggage.

Go over it in every minute detail (smell it, feel it, taste it). Smile at the memory of it. Let the joy of it flood your whole mind, brain, and body.

Now open your eyes and refocus on something that makes you feel good.

Come out of the cave exercise

(you can find this online at The Talking Room)

Close your eyes and breathe down into your tummy.

Open the inner eye into your imagination and imagine that you are up the back of the cave.

It's dark, dank, but safe. BOB, the survival brain wants you to stay here, away from threats or harm (physical or emotional).

Come out from the back of the cave towards the entrance, where you can see there's sunshine outside, and people are out there playing, working, having fun. Even though it's scary, go up to the entrance to the cave and look out. Any tigers? Nope. Any enemies? Nope. Smell the fresh air and the sunshine. Take as long as you like to go through the cave entrance. Feel the sunshine, and the breeze on your skin. People come up to you and stroke you (physically or emotionally). You feel free and safe. Do this as many times as is necessary to get yourself out there in the sunshine.

Physical exercise

At the very least, if you can, walk for 20 to 30 minutes once a day

Anything more than this is a great bonus.

Do Housework.

Garden.

Walk around your office building.

Stand up at your desk – ask for a standing desk.

Move.

Acknowledgements

I would like to thank my family, especially my husband, Russell Searle, and my daughter, Aimee Cooper, for their support and practical help.

I want to thank members of the Peninsula Writers' Club and other readers who read the book and gave me feedback, especially Sue Boundy, Sue Croft, Jeanette Woods, Liz Hicklin, and Sue Broberg. Also, Ally Jaks.

Thanks to my writing buddy and mentor, Robert Gott.

Special thanks to Rob Gerrand of Norstrilia Press for believing in the book.

If I've left anyone out, I'm probably in the shit, but I'm not giving one.

Bibliography, References and Further Reading

Books with asterisks *** are 'easy reads'

'Train your mind change your brain': Sharon Begley ***

'The mind and the brain: neuroplasticity and the power of mental force': Jeffrey M. Schwartz, M.D. and Sharon Begley

'You are not your brain': Dr Jeffrey Schwartz and Rebecca Gladding

'The brain that changes itself': Norman Doidge *** (and 'The brain's way of healing')

'Mindfulness and acceptance: Expanding the Cognitive-Behavioural Tradition': Edited by Steven C. Hayes, Victoria M. Follette and Marsha M Linehan

The Happiness Trap' by Dr Russ Harris *** (plus 'The Happiness Trap Handbook)

'Mindfulness for life': Dr Stephen McKenzie and Dr Craig Hassad ***

'Know your mind' – Everyday Emotional and Psychological Problems and How to Overcome Them': Dr Daniel Freeman and Jason Freeman ***

'Being a brain-wise therapist' - A Practical Guide to Interpersonal Neurobiology: Bonnie Badenoch

'Emotional intelligence': Daniel Goleman (Also 'Social Intelligence' and 'Intelligence at work'

'my stroke of insight'- A Brain Scientist's Personal Journey: Jill Bolte Taylor PhD plus http://www.ted.com/talks/jill_bolte_taylor_s_ powerful_stroke_of_insight.html ***

'Feeling good, The New Mood Therapy': David D. Burns, M.D. ***

'Change your thinking – Positive and practical ways to overcome stress, negative emotions and self-defeating behaviour using CBT': Sarah Edelman PhD ***

'Positive psychology, The Science of Happiness and Human Strengths': Alan Carr

'Learned optimism': Martin Seligman, PhD

'Relief without drugs, how you can Overcome Tension, Anxiety and Pain': Ainslie Meares, M.D. *** (particularly first half)

'Walking With Cavemen' DVD Series, BBC: 'Becoming Human' Series, SBS ***

'Sapiens': by Yuval Noah Harari (also available in graphic form)

'The Polyvagal Theory Neurophysiological Foundations of Emotions, Attachment, Communication, Self-regulation': Stephen W. Porges

'The 10 Best-ever Depression Management Techniques': Margaret Wehrenberg

'The Food-mood Solution All-Natural Ways to Banish Anxiety, Depression, Anger, Stress, Overeating and Alcohol and Drug Problems – and Feel Good Again': Jack Challem ***

'Potatoes Not Prozac': Kathleen Desmaisons PhD ***

'Magnificent Mind at Any Age': Daniel C. Amen, M.D. ***

A Primer of Freudian Psychology': Calvin S. Hall ***

'Memories, Dreams, Reflections': C.G. Jung ***

'Why Men Don't Listen, And Women Can't Read

Maps – How we're different and what to do about it: Allan and Barbara Pease ***

'The Definitive Book of Body Language – How to read other's attitudes by their gestures: Allan and Barbara Pease ***

'Your Body Language Shapes Who You Are' and 'Power Posing, How The Body Changes The Mind' Amy Cuddy, Harvard Business School. TED talks, YouTube ***

'Man's Search For Meaning': Viktor E. Frankl ***

'The Addictive Personality, Understanding the Addictive Process and Compulsive Behaviour: Craig Nakken ***

'Set Yourself Free' – Breaking the cycle of co-dependency and compulsive addictive behaviour: Shirley Smith PhD ***

'The Highly Sensitive Person': Elaine Aron ***

'Creative Visualization – Use the Power of Your Imagination to Create What You Want in Your Life': Shakti Gawain ***

'Be Like Water, Practical Wisdom from the Martial Arts': Joseph Cardillo ***

'The Art of Being and Becoming': Hazrat Inayat Khan ***

The Way of Zen: Alan Watts – Any one of a multitude on talks on YouTube by Alan Watts psychologist and philosopher ***

Some Sayings of The Buddha According to The Pali Canon: Translated by F.L. Woodward

Meditations: Marcus Aurelius: Translated by Gregory Hays ***

The Tao Te Ching: Lao Tzu: Translated by Stephen Mitchell ***

Profanity Can be as Therapeutic AF – Dan Mager,

author of *Some Assembly Required: A Balanced Approach to Recovery from Addiction and Chronic Pain* and *Roots and Wings*

https://www.psychologytoday.com/au/blog/some-assembly-required/201801/profanity-can-be-therapeutic-af